Ahead Of The Curve

Graham Leslie CBE

How I Became The Disruptor

GREAT NORTHERN

Great Northern Books
PO Box 1380, Bradford,
West Yorkshire, BD5 5FB

www.greatnorthernbooks.co.uk

© Graham Leslie/Andy Hirst 2024

Every effort has been made to acknowledge
correctly and contact the copyright holders
of material in this book. Great Northern
Books Ltd apologises for any unintentional
errors or omissions, which should be
notified to the publisher.

All rights reserved. No part of this book
may be reproduced in any form or by any
means without permission in writing from
the publisher, except by a reviewer who
may quote brief passages in a review.

ISBN: 978-1-914227-68-4

Design by David Burrill

CIP Data
A catalogue for this book is available from
the British Library

This book has been created as my small token of total love and appreciation of my mother and father, Anne and Hugh Leslie, brother Hugh and sister Annette, all my children, stepchildren and grandchildren and my eternal gratitude to the undying loyal love and support of Mrs Karen Michelle Leslie, the third and last.

It's also dedicated to the millions of people worldwide who give their time without cost as volunteers to charities as, without those people, millions would suffer.

Graham

Graham Leslie

Graham Leslie went from living in a council house to meeting American presidents, British prime ministers and members of the royal family, and along the way created Galpharm International Ltd – one of the most pioneering pharmaceutical companies the UK has ever seen, and which has saved the NHS more than £400m every year since 1995.

He was founder chairman and creator of the first all-seater sports stadium in the UK, the Huddersfield stadium that became the forerunner for modern stadium design, including Wembley.

He is currently creating the world's first AI app for young musicians to distribute their music globally.

Graham is one of the UK's most respected entrepreneurs, philanthropists and business innovators, and here he tells his incredible life story, sharing some of the secrets of his great success.

It is an inspirational 'rags to riches' tale, about a man with a big smile and an even bigger heart, who has achieved so much against the odds.

Andy Hirst

Graham's autobiography has been ghostwritten by respected Yorkshire journalist Andy Hirst, who has more than thirty years' experience in the media industry and now runs his own business AH! PR (www.ah-pr.com) specialising in ghostwriting, press releases, blogging, website content, copywriting and award applications.

Making Waves

All proceeds from the book are going to the charity Making Waves which is the charitable side to the Waves day centre in Slaithwaite, Huddersfield, and takes members from Huddersfield, Kirklees and across West Yorkshire.

Waves is one of the most innovative day centres in the UK, helping people aged 18 and over with learning and/or physical difficulties to lead full lives with activities including performing arts, baking, making music, arts and crafts, virtual reality games, swimming, walks, horticulture, caring for animals, holidays and sharing what they do on social media.

The charity supports the centre and also provides respite care and overnight breaks when members' families face a crisis.

Andy Hirst's son, George, was a member at Waves and loved being there before sadly passing away in July 2021, aged just 27.

Find out more about Waves and Making Waves at www.wavesgroup.co.uk or access it through this QR code.

You can make a donation to Making Waves at their Just Giving page, accessed via this QR Code.

Thank you ... for everything

First of all thank you to everyone who has bought this autobiography which is raising money for such a great cause.

I've visited the Waves day centre and the quality of life it provides for people with disabilities is phenomenal. There are so many charities out there doing wonderful things for their communities, so please try to support any you can.

Family is everything and that was taught to me from birth by my parents, Hugh and Anne, who showed passion, honesty, respect and love for each other and this bond still continues deeply today between me, my sister Annette and brother Hugh and their children.

Thank you to my wives Sandra, Ann and now Karen, who have shared so much with me on life's journey which has certainly had its challenging times as well as some great ones.

To my four children, Craig, Amanda, Alex and Fay – I'm so proud of you all – and also to my three stepchildren, Matthew and Thomas Brooke and Lucy Williams for their excellent and loyal support.

Thanks so much for providing me with my wonderful grandchildren.

To everyone who has helped me in business over the years, especially the brilliant team we had at Galpharm. We simply wouldn't have had the success without you. I like to read inspirational quotes and sayings but there really is no 'i' in team and life is all about teamwork.

Thanks to the University of Huddersfield which made me a professor so I could try to inspire their students who will be the entrepreneurs of the future. Not bad for a lad who left school with dyslexia and no formal qualifications with 'could do better' ringing in his ears.

Thanks to all those who supported me through the tough times at Huddersfield Town – times when the club could well have gone out of business until the stadium became its beacon of hope.

Look where the club is now with a stadium that still looks as space-age as it did back then, exactly 30 years ago. Enjoy every moment watching the Terriers – an afternoon at football can take you through the full range of life's emotions and passions.

A sincere thank you to everyone who has contributed photos,

particularly the ones from The Huddersfield Daily Examiner and the University of Huddersfield, and words, especially all the lovely comments at the back which I've found very moving.

Thanks to my second wife, Ann, an excellent photographer who developed all her own photographs like the one on the back cover that she took in 1977 of me playing my guitar.

My final thank you is the one that means everything to me and it's to Karen. You are the world to me and with all your love, patience, support and brilliant organisational skills you make every day special.

Graham Leslie, Spring 2024

Special thanks to our sponsors and all who helped on the book

A big thanks to everyone who kindly gave their time for the book and agreed to be interviewed.

Also David Burrill, creative director at Great Northern Books, who had faith in the project by believing my story was one worth telling.

The following sponsors have all made donations to Making Waves. A huge thanks to them all.

Ramsdens Solicitors, Huddersfield

BHP accountants and tax advisors, Sheffield

Yorkshire Country Properties, Bradford

JPB Jewellery, Huddersfield

Hair Tools, Ravensthorpe (David and Alison Brunton)

Kirsty Franks Marketing, Wakefield

The Parish live music venue in Huddersfield (Tom Simpson)

Grange Moor Garage, Grange Moor and Honley, Huddersfield

Approved Food, Barnsley

Handelsbanken relationship bank, Bradley, Huddersfield

G&T Accountancy Services, Denby Dale, Huddersfield

AJ Bell pension and investment advisors, Manchester

Fantastic Media, Leeds (Andy Hobson)

Andrew Mansell and family

Film Buddy, Armitage Bridge, Huddersfield (Ben Sweet and family)

Ian Uttley and family

David Dyson and family

TSL Healthcare, Wakefield (Chris Patterson and family)

David Pitts and family

Innerva power assisted exercise technology, Honley (Howard Blackburn and family)

CIGA Healthcare in Northern Ireland (Irwin Armstrong and family)

Mike and Jacqui Volf and family, including first grandchild Theo

The Woodman Inn, Thunderbridge, Huddersfield

Julie and Simon Dedman and family

Kieran and Helen O'Regan

Lee Henton and family

Jim and Margaret Douglas and family

Picturedrome in Holmfirth (Peter Carr and family)

Paxman Scalp Cooling, Fenay Bridge, Huddersfield

Smile Bar and Venue, Huddersfield (Richard and Marie Harrison)

Hinchliffe Holmes estate agents in Cheshire

Da Sandro Italian restaurant, Birchencliffe, Huddersfield

Sentinel Investment Group, Cheshire

A chance for you to win a fantastic prize

We want this autobiography to be a great read and also a fun one too.

So we've set three questions and the winner will have a personal painting done for them by internationally-renowned royal artist Richard Gower who is featured in the book. It's a prize worth thousands of pounds.

1. There is an inspirational story in the book which is totally made up, but, to give you two clues, there is a moral behind it and it's not in the chapter called 'The strange way I met Bill Clinton … and some other great Graham tales.' You'll need to read most of the book to find it.

2. The wage bill for the entire Huddersfield Town squad in 1992/93 came to just short of £8,500 a week and had such names as Phil Starbuck, Iwan Roberts, Simon Charlton and Iffy Onuora in it, with trainees on just £29.50 a week. But can you guess how much the highest paid player at the time, captain Peter Jackson, was earning each week?

3. Ex-Irish international Kieran O'Regan was also a highly popular player in 1992/93 so guess how much he was earning every week too. The clue is he was on less than Jacko!

The person who gets the first question spot on and is nearest to the second and third answers will win. If it's a tie then it's the first one pulled from the hat. Deadline for entries is Friday, 25 October 2024.

Email your answers along with your name and phone number to andy@ah-pr.com

Contents

Preface 15
I defied Hitler simply by being born 17
It's grim up north 20
Schooldays aren't necessarily the best days of your life 23
Heading for the catwalk ... or possibly not 31
Goodbye Graham ... hello André 33
Settling down with Sandra 38
Hello Huddersfield 41
Life on the dole ... but things can only get better 44
How my pharmaceutical career was almost over before it began .. 47
The day Sir Stanley Matthews ran rings round me 50
Getting going with Galpharm 55
Galpharm starts to grow with weird things happening
along the way 63
Whisky, women and razor blades with a couple of
Peaky Blinders moments 68
The day I flew with the world's dodgiest pilot 73
How buying some razors ended up with a police raid 75
How the danger of 'passing off' was cheekily ahead of the curve ... 79
The memorable day Galpharm really took off 80
Why I rejected $11m for Galpharm, but was it the right decision? 86
How I almost lost my new-found fortune 89
The day I joined the Huddersfield Town board ...
and instantly knew things had to change 94
Why the stadium had to be more than just a football arena 101
Town gets a reluctant new chairman ... me 108
Why I just had to have the Galpharm name on the first ever
purpose-built all-seater stadium in the UK 112

My tips on how to do well in business 115

Loving helping businesses ...
but sometimes it doesn't quite work out 117

Why helping others is in the blood 123

The Leslie Business Barometer ...
how to keep moving forward in business 129

My businesses close to home 134

How the University of Huddersfield ended up with its first
non-academic Resident Professor of Enterprise and
Entrepreneurship 141

The strange way I met Bill Clinton ...
and some other great Graham tales 145

Businesses I'm helping now and future plans 152

Why everyone should help charities ...
and how charities can help themselves 154

What family means to me 158

From Austin 10 to racing around Le Mans in a
brand-new Bentley 161

My love of nature and art 166

Little drummer boy ends up taking music to a global level 169

Great quotes and sayings that have inspired me 175

Afterwords 178

In this final section of the book others have their say on Graham, starting with what his family thinks

Graham's Huddersfield Town and stadium years ... here are the thoughts of stadium architect Rod Sheard, Sir John Harman, Paul Fletcher, Andy Booth, Peter Jackson, Steve Kindon, Kieran O'Regan, Ann Hough, Andy Hobson, Mel Booth and John Gledhill

The Galpharm years ... business associates lift the lid on working with Graham

What the academics think of Professor Graham Leslie at the University of Huddersfield

People Graham has helped over the years share their thoughts

Preface

It's said the bumble bee has no right to fly.

Aerodynamically, due to its body weight and limited wingspan, it should never even get off the ground, yet the bee not only flies but is super productive throughout its entire life.

Like the bee, on paper Graham Leslie should never have become a multi-millionaire entrepreneur and philanthropist.

He left school with no recognised qualifications after an academic life blighted by dyslexia and came from a financially poor middle-class background.

But he had values instilled in him by parents who had endured poverty, trauma and hardship and those qualities gave him the confidence, determination and never-say-die spirit to fly, whatever the odds stacked against him. Rather like the bumble bee.

Graham built one of the UK's biggest and best-known pharmaceutical companies, Galpharm, from scratch, which made medicines affordable and readily available for millions of people while saving the NHS £400m a year.

He was also chairman of Huddersfield Town Football Club in the early 1990s, saving both it and Huddersfield Rugby League Club from administration.

Graham then had the vision, drive and determination to kick-start the project that led to a new stadium in Huddersfield, becoming founder chairman of Kirklees Stadium Development Ltd, and the stadium was designed and built incredibly quickly in just two years.

The stadium was so striking and different it set the standards for all other UK sports grounds to follow, inspired the new Wembley stadium and is the only stadium to ever win architecture's top prize when it was named Building of the Year in 1995 by the Royal Institute of British Architects.

That's why the autobiography's title is *Ahead Of The Curve*. The stadium's famous design with its innovative banana-shaped trusses threw a curve ball into stadium design, but Graham has constantly been a disruptor, often doing things differently to everyone else.

Since selling Galpharm for $86m in 2008, Graham has gone on to help countless other businesses and charities, earning a CBE in 2017 for his philanthropy and ceaseless entrepreneurial spirit.

In a way this book asks what is an entrepreneur? People who have created a successful business should, quite rightly, be regarded as enterprising, but a true entrepreneur is someone who is successful in business time and time again. An entrepreneur is an innovator and, sometimes, a disruptor too because they change how people think by the totally new way they've done something.

A philanthropist uses experience, influence, connections and wealth to help the community and charities and also coaches other businesses for no personal gain. The most valuable assets they can give is their time and wisdom.

Graham Leslie is all these – an entrepreneur, a philanthropist, a connector, an innovator and a disruptor.

Here Graham tells his life story with honesty and humour, revealing how he's sometimes been lucky to survive both physically and financially, sometimes when everything seemed to be against him.

He reveals his early days as a hairdresser in the 1960s, how a twist of fate led him into the pharmaceutical industry, his time as a racing driver in the 1990s, the businesses he has helped, his undying passion for music – including how he wrote a song for La Toya Jackson – and his plans to change the music industry in the future.

All this and Graham also shares tips on how to be successful in business, including how to double your profits in a year.

In a special section of the book many people who have known Graham over the years, including some of Huddersfield Town's most legendary footballers, also share their thoughts on the man and the enigma that is Graham Leslie.

PS: Graham has told many stories as video pods lasting a couple of minutes each. To see them and his music go to his website www.grahamleslie.co.uk or use these QR codes.

I defied Hitler simply by being born

If Hitler had his way I'd never have been born.

My parents were both Glaswegians who moved to London when Dad joined the Probation Service. As it turned out, he couldn't have chosen a more momentous or notorious year in history to do it – 1939, the year the Second World War broke out.

My dad, Hugh, joined the Royal Artillery and was away for the next five years serving in India, defending the country from the Japanese who were rampaging through Burma. If they had reached India, the British forces were so ill-equipped that it's likely they'd have been massacred. He was always bitter that they were the forgotten army during World War Two.

He joined on December 12, 1940 and was away training before sailing for Bombay in May 1941 and didn't return to these shores until October 1945 before finally being demobbed as a sergeant in April 1946. He was lucky to survive as he was on a ship sailing to help British forces in Singapore just before it fell to the Japanese in February 1942, but his troopship was torpedoed and so limped back to her original base.

My mum, Anne, and their only child at the time, Annette, were left at home in Dagenham, East London. Mum was only 22 – Dad was eight years older – so in effect she became a single mother during the war but still did her bit for the war effort, working at the Admiralty.

She had Annette in 1941 after Hugh had left for India, but the London hospital where she'd been due to give birth had been bombed and badly damaged so a friend of Dad's drove her up to a temporary hospital in Hitchin, Hertfordshire, which had been converted from an old workhouse.

Life must have been terrifying. Dagenham was high on the Luftwaffe's target list as it had munitions factories and was also seen as an important transport hub. It was raided several times and one night a piece of shrapnel from a bomb flew through Mum's bedroom window at her house on Dunkeld Road, narrowly missing both her and Annette. Mum kept that 'lucky' piece of shrapnel.

Annette remembers going to the Anderson shelter during the bombing but didn't feel fear as Mum was always with her to keep her feeling safe. For her first five years Annette never met her father and only knew him through letters and drawings he sent from India. At one point the letters stopped for six months as the ship they were on was torpedoed and sank.

Every day was tough and as the war years went on both Mum and Annette suffered from malnutrition as there simply wasn't enough to eat, but the neighbours there were amazing despite constantly living on the edge of despair, destruction and death.

She didn't see Dad for five years and when he returned early in November 1945 he walked straight into the house and thought at first no-one was home.

Then he heard a splash of water, went to investigate and found Mum treating herself to something she did exceptionally rarely … having a bath. Within seconds Dad was in with her, making up for five years of frustrating separation with several minutes of intense passion.

Nine months to the day I was born within the sound of Bow Bells so I'm a true cockney. I often wonder if the passion that created me was what gave me the drive, the determination and the unquenchable desire to succeed.

I'd like to think it did, especially as Mum dropped a bombshell when I was 45. I was actually born a twin but, tragically, my brother or sister didn't survive childbirth.

That's how it was in those days. Tragedy in the 1940s was everywhere, virtually every family suffered it and death was accepted as part of daily life. You just had to get on with it.

Although my full name is Graham Andrew Leslie, I actually should never have been called Graham. I was supposed to be a Brian. Dad was dispatched to register my birth in Dagenham with orders from Mum to name me Brian Andrew.

Perhaps all the years standing next to huge artillery guns being fired had damaged his hearing, but he was convinced she'd said Graham Andrew and then made yet another mistake by not even using the Scottish spelling of Graeme. So my name became Graham Andrew Leslie and Dad was never allowed to forget the mistake he'd made, constantly getting rollicked for messing up registering my birth.

A classic case of 'you only had one job to do … and you couldn't even get that right.'

Still, I think Graham's way better than Brian as a name.

Mum was a stunning, beautiful woman who loved music, dancing and entertaining while Dad was far more regimented and disciplined in everything he did, but both had a phenomenal sense of humour.

Dad was born in the Gorbals area of Glasgow in August 1910 – an area of slum tenements notorious for the harshness of life there. He was the seventh child of the seventh child and lost two of his siblings who died young, which Dad later described as 'from poverty and neglect'. He worked as a salesman in a tailor's but educated himself to have a better career and in the evenings was a volunteer PT instructor in the Boys' Brigade.

Mum was born on Scotland's favourite night of the year – New Year's Eve – in 1917 near the famous Glasgow Cross that marks the city centre. She was the only surviving child of Maggie McColl who worked all her life to support her child after her husband, a police officer in Glasgow, died from pneumonia when Mum was only three or four.

Life was bleak in the city. Gang warfare was rife and hundreds of children were losing their fathers to the nightmare slaughter in the First World War trenches. Both my parents lost their fathers before they were even born, but they met after Dad joined the Glasgow 2nd Battalion Boys' Brigade and Mum the Girls' Life Brigade, forging a life built on the ultimate respect they always had for one another.

Both had an exceptionally strong Christian faith and were members of the Church of Scotland. They had three children, me, Annette and younger brother Hugh. We all thought the world of them and they were together for more than 50 years.

They had an overwhelming sense of right and wrong and would always fight for what they believed in. Mum supported the suffragettes battling for women to have the vote and once chained herself to railings in Glasgow. That's when Dad was sure she was the one for him.

Together they brought such unity to the family, along with enormous love and joy and set high standards for all three of us to follow, and we've been forever grateful to them that they did that.

When I was five Dad got a job as the principal probation officer in Middlesbrough. Life was just about to get a whole lot tougher in the North East, but over the next 15 years I discovered the truth in the saying that 'what doesn't break you, makes you stronger.'

No-one was ever going to break me. Ever.

It's grim up north

We moved to the North East in the bleak midwinter of 1951 to Middlesbrough which I quickly came to simply call The Boro.

The journey there from Dagenham was a tad traumatic as Middlesbrough was in the county of North Yorkshire at the time and as we drove towards it from the south we eventually hit the moors which were covered in deep snow piled several feet high on both sides of what we could still see of the road.

There were three things of note on the moors that day – a lady school teacher walking home, a washing line and a telegraph pole. Dad managed to somehow hit all three as he slithered and skidded slowly along. Fortunately the lady was hurt far less than Dad's pride. We managed to plough on, quite literally, through the blizzard and I was so relieved when we made it safe and sound to our little council house at 25 Manton Avenue.

We lived in a council house because Dad was badly paid even though he held such a high and responsible job in the Probation Service. That's how it was in those days.

It was a terraced house with arched alleyways leading to the back gardens and one of my first memories of life there was a street party for the Queen's Coronation on June 2, 1953. The memories were not so much the tables laid out with food nor the bunting fluttering in the breeze but the fact that so many kids were out playing in their vests … and I mean just their vests and nothing else.

The only heating in the house was the open fire – this was a long time before the luxury of central heating – and we used to joke we were kept warm by Dad sucking on a peppermint and then breathing on us.

We had a sitting room and a dining room. Mum and Dad hated the word lounge as they reckoned only pubs had lounges and as both were teetotal neither bothered stepping inside them.

There was no TV, of course. I used to amuse myself by forever playing out and when a family six doors down was the first to get a black and white TV with a tiny screen they suddenly became incredibly popular on the street.

We later moved to number 10 Asterley Drive at Acklam in Middlesbrough, a neat three-bedroom semi-detached and we introduced Hogmanay to the street. It was a double celebration with my mum's birthday also being on New Year's Eve. The front door was opened on the stroke of midnight so the 'first footers' could step across the threshold. Custom has it that the first person stepping in set the tone for the year ahead and is always welcomed with traditional Scottish hospitality in the shape of a dram of whisky. Visitors were supposed to bring a gift and a traditional one was a piece of coal to represent warmth but nowadays it's more likely to be a bottle of booze.

The first year my parents did it only a couple of neighbours turned up, but word got round and the house was rammed the second year, so much so that I can remember my mum cooking the visitors breakfast at 7am as some of them were still there. It's not like they didn't have homes to go to ... they all lived on our street.

At that time Middlesbrough attracted people from all over the world to work in its two industries – the ICI chemical plant or the Dorman and Long steelworks which could trace its roots back to 1875 and was once listed on the London Stock Exchange. Dorman and Long were steel makers, construction engineers and bridge builders who constructed many of the most famous bridges built in the late 1920s and early 1930s, including the Sydney Harbour Bridge, the Tyne Bridge and the Tees Transporter Bridge.

The local folk even regarded the incoming workers from the UK as 'foreigners' as they made the trek to find work in the north from Scotland, Wales, Ireland and, God forbid, Lancashire and even London. Times were hard, people had to work to live and they had to go wherever that work was, no matter where that might be. Middlesbrough was a northern powerhouse 90 years before the phrase was even invented.

The 1950s are now a rapidly fading era for many, but life was tougher and simpler then. Early memories include going to church and then listening to larger-than-life cockney band leader Billy Cotton's Wakey Wakey Radio Show as we ate our roast Sunday dinner. This was occasionally followed, at Mum's request, by a trip out in the car to the east coast to Redcar or Saltburn where Dad had done his pre-war military training before he was posted to India. I'm not sure that Saltburn was particularly realistic training for what awaited him in India, but there you go.

In summer when we went to the beach we wore swimsuits knitted by Mum and for a while mine had an A emblazoned on it. Looking at a picture of me in it now, people are puzzled why it's an A. The simple explanation is that it was a hand-me-down from my older sister, Annette, hence the A which Mum had stitched on her costume.

It was still very much the era of 'make do and mend' so Mum taught me how to sew, darn socks and knit and she cut up old pairs of Dad's trousers to make me a pair. She even had a go at teaching me how to use her typewriter, which was more of a struggle considering I was dyslexic yet had never heard of the word or even the condition back in those days.

We had to queue up to get bottles of orange juice as it was still rationed after the war and the Government gave we little ones something for nowt ... free school milk.

It was a society based on respect. If I walked past our doctor, teacher or minister in the street I was expected to tip my school cap. Woe betide me if I didn't.

Life was all about character building but perhaps what forged my character at such an early age was something my parents made me do ... something so terrible it still haunts me to this day. They provided me with a bike put together with bits of scrap scrounged from Westwood's scrapyard – all good so far – but then enrolled me on Scottish country dancing classes, supposedly to help keep their Scottish heritage alive.

This meant I had to ride through Middlesbrough on Saturdays wearing a kilt to get to my lessons where my dance partner was a girl called Penny Lamb. I was 14 by then so you can imagine the ridicule, the torment and even the beatings I endured because of that kilt as I pedalled my way to the dancing school at Park Presbyterian Church Hall on Linthorpe Road as fast as I could to get the ride over as quickly as possible.

I was once knocked off my bike when a driver opened his car door without looking and then apologised profusely, thinking he'd hurt a young girl.

"Are you OK, love?" he said.

I stood up and said 'yes' and a look of horror crossed his face when he realised I was a lad in a kilt. He called me a 'puff', got back into his car muttering to himself and then drove off swearing.

That's growing up in the 1950s for you.

Schooldays aren't necessarily the best days of your life

My schooldays started in 1951 and finished in 1962 at Whinney Banks Infant, Junior and then Secondary Modern School, for me a foreboding-looking brick-built school with two large wings on either side of a massive clock tower – one side for the girls and the other for the boys.

It looked more like a Willy Wonka-style factory than a school. I was there for 10 years in all from the age of five to 15 and felt imprisoned in it. I can remember the green and black school tie and having to wear shorts, even in deep midwinter. And you tell kids that today ...

My academic learning never really got up and running, it kind of more meandered around a bit. I disliked the system, struggled with some of the lessons and regarded my main role as the class clown, out to entertain all my classmates.

My struggle with subjects such as English, science and maths – either due to my as yet undiagnosed dyslexia or inability to understand what on earth they were on about – saw me often sent out of the class. Now that became something of a bonus as I'd learned to love nature and was enthralled watching birds nesting, bees making honey, the flowers gently swaying in the wind – in short, nature in all its glory – especially in a pond in a quadrangle which separated the boys from the girls.

When I did bunk off school a bloke on a bike we knew as the 'school bobby' would go searching and then drag me back into the classroom. He was good at his job too and knew all the usual hiding haunts.

Then I had to face the academic nightmare of the 11-plus exam which my elder sister, Annette, had sailed through. I, on the other hand, sank without trace. As an August baby I was always among the very youngest in the class and that, coupled with my natural dislike for all things school, scuppered my 11-plus chances.

I seem to remember that one of the questions was: 'What's the lightest, a ton of feathers or a ton of bricks?' I fell for it and put a ton of bricks, thinking they must be heavier. Duh!

I put my own spin on it when I handed Mum the brown envelope containing my disappointing results.

"Everything will be fine, Mum," I said. "Don't worry, I'll be staying at the same school."

I'm not sure my reassuring words really worked as she immediately burst into tears.

What had made it worse was that I'd had an IQ test before the exams which put me at 165 and Annette at 158 – or that may have been the other way round – so my parents naturally assumed I'd walk the 11-plus. They assumed wrongly as I was tripped up by my nervousness in the exam room and the fact that the subjects I did well in such as sport and woodwork were not on the 11-plus radar.

So I failed, which was a word I grew up to detest as nobody fails, it's just that at times we don't quite succeed. It's a kinder, far less derogatory way of looking at it and gives more natural encouragement to try and do better next time. So, to put a positive twist on it, let's just say I successfully duffed my 11-plus.

This meant I was stuck at Whinney Banks for another four years, a place I used to unaffectionately refer to as 'the asylum'.

One thing I did excel at was dodging difficult questions – usually with cheeky one-line retorts – which stood me in good stead for my future working life as a salesman. I may have pushed the boundaries as something of a maverick and I suppose could even be naughty at times but me and my friends were never aggressive or bullying.

For some reason this incident sticks in my mind.

There were twins at the school called David and John Swift and one day they had a huge red see-through lolly on a stick – the kind you get at fairs.

One of them held the lolly out and said to me: "Would you like a lick?"

"Sure," I replied, but when I stuck my tongue out he snatched the lolly away and said: "Well, you can't have one."

Trouble was, he then tried it with Big Daft Dave and when he told him he wasn't having a lick Dave snatched it away from him, broke the lolly in two, smashed it on the ground and stood on it before turning to the twins and saying: "Well, neither can you."

That was them told.

Discipline was tough and no-nonsense at the school. Step out of line and you'd be caned, so most kids decided discretion was the better part of valour and so conformed.

I also had a hardworking ethos by the age of 12 or 13, getting up at 5.30am to deliver milk in the Brookfield area and then straight onto a paper round by 7am before off to school on the bus. I felt I learned more on the milk round and paper round – especially communicating with people – than I ever did at school.

I was good at sport, especially football and athletics, helped by the fact my sister was going out with the British and European one mile champion at the time, Trevor Schofield. I represented the school at town and county levels in all sports and even had a decent go at trying to get into the girls' rounders team as they used to let me join in at lunchtimes. Life wasn't as inclusive then and I wasn't allowed in the team, probably due to my hairy legs.

I enjoyed woodwork, metalwork and geography but struggled with science, maths and history and, as for English, that may as well have been a foreign language, not helped by the Geordie accents, my parents' strong Scottish accents and dyslexia really starting to kick in as school life rolled along.

No-one knew what dyslexia was in the late 1950s and so I'd get caned in class for not reading properly and told off at home to the point that Dad would hit me round the head with the reading book when he got so frustrated with my attempts to stumble through each page or, even worse, I'd ad lib and make it up.

I just about managed the Peter and Jane story books but anything beyond that was beyond me.

It also meant my spelling was poor and, although I tend to get all the right letters involved, they're often not necessarily in the right order and I still spell quite as quiet to this day every time.

I've only ever read two books from front to back and they were *Lady Chatterley's Lover* and *The Life and Times of Mariano Fortuny y Madrazo* – both for reasons which will soon become very clear.

For some bizarre reason the school thought it would be a great idea to appoint me as the prompt in the school play, following the action in the script and then helping the ultra-nervous young actors with their lines if they forgot them. I was soon sacked from the role when it became blindingly obvious I couldn't read anywhere near well enough to keep up with what was happening on stage. It was like there was some kind of barrier between my eyes and my brain. I could see the words but my brain struggled to process them.

My parents then had the bright idea that Barnard Castle boarding school would sort me out so arranged for me to sit a 13-plus entrance exam. The school wanted me for my sporting prowess and the entrance exam to get into this 'posh asylum' was a magnificent 13%. Only a blithering idiot would fail it, surely.

Step forward Graham Andrew Leslie who deliberately messed it up even to the point of spelling his own name wrong.

Needless to say my parents were distraught and the journey home was in deathly silence until my dad eventually stated the blindingly obvious by saying in a stern voice: "You didn't want to go there, did you?"

I replied: "Well, I would have done if all my friends could have come with me."

That didn't help the situation or the silence although my 18-year-old sister was happy enough as she'd spent the day being escorted around the school by the handsome head boy.

If I'd actually got a place there I've no idea how my parents would have been able to afford the fees so it was probably for the best all round that I flunked it.

The next week I was back at Whinney Banks with another year-and-a-half to complete before I'd escape into the big wide world of supposedly endless opportunity.

The headmaster, Mr Reid, was a friend of my parents and he was such a wonderfully gentle, fair but firm Christian man that he was affectionately known as Pop Reid. He saw something in me because he made me a prefect and then promoted me to head boy in 1960 and captain of Durham House.

I'd got the top posts, so what could possibly go wrong before my final exams? Actually, plenty, and proved the old saying that pride comes before a fall.

I would have expected the problems to come from humourless geography teacher Mr Gasgarth, although there may be some justification in retrospect for his dour demeanour. He'd lost a leg in the Second World War when a troop-carrying ship he was on was sunk by a torpedo and the pupils called him 'peg leg' and often walked past him singing 'Peggy Sue'.

Unsurprisingly, he had a short temper and, if you misbehaved or even looked like you were going to misbehave, a solid-wood board rubber would come heading your way ... usually at head height. The trick then was to open your desk top at just the right moment to deflect it so it hit someone else.

To be fair, he loved his subject and was the most respected teacher in the school.

As it was, the incident happened in history teacher Mr Thomas's class. He was tall, thin, gaunt, very boring and struggled to keep his pupils under control.

One day a boy sitting in front of me stood up to answer a question but when he went to sit down the boy next to me had pushed his chair to the side so the hapless victim landed with a loud thump on the floor and yelled out in shock and pain.

Mr Thomas shouted: "Leslie, come out here."

"But it wasn't me," I replied. "Sir, you've got it wrong."

He was in no mood to listen and threatened to report me to the headmaster if I didn't step forward to take my punishment – six of the best with his cane.

Reluctantly, I walked to the front and had to hold my hand out while Mr Thomas took his cane from his desk, lifted it high and then brought it smashing down on my hand. The pain immediately shot up my arm and registered in my head where my brain thought: "Wow, that blooming hurt."

He chose my left so I could still write with my right. He brought the cane down twice more with welts starting to immediately appear on the skin.

He raised the cane again to administer a fourth blow but I'd had enough and in my red mist grabbed the cane, yanked it from his hand and bent it so angrily and forcibly it snapped in two. That's not an easy thing to do as canes, by their very nature, are there to give some stick and are incredibly pliable.

Mr Thomas was in a state of shock as the 30 boys in the class began to clap and chant my name as though I was some kind of comic book hero straight out of the pages of *The Dandy* or *The Beano*.

Panic then set in and I turned and left the room before walking out of school.

I returned the next day, hailed as a hero by my classmates and a villain by the teachers who exacted their revenge by caning me again … this time in front of the whole school at assembly and I was stripped of my role as house captain.

Years later I discovered that the caning may have been Mr Thomas's way of taking revenge on my dad for his role of chief probation officer. Turns out Mr Thomas had to report regularly to the probation office – once a fortnight – but no-one knew why. It must have really rankled with him.

Nationally, the times were slowly starting to change, no more so than when a highly publicised court case finished on November 2, 1960, deciding that *Lady Chatterley's Lover* written by DH Lawrence in the 1920s was no longer obscene. The case was the first prosecution of a work of literary merit under the Obscene Publications Act 1959 and the publication of *Lady Chatterley's Lover* was a shrewd move by Penguin to test the new law, 30 years after Lawrence's death.

They were so sure they'd win they had already printed 200,000 copies ready to go as soon as the case was over to make the most of its intense glare of publicity. When they won they sold two million copies in the UK within a month.

The novice entrepreneur that was Graham Leslie decided to get in on the act. Even at that age I'd been impressed by Penguin's 'balls of steel'. The court case was the perfect gamble that had paid off spectacularly.

The case started on October 20, 1960, at the Old Bailey and I heard some dockers in Middlesbrough had copies of the banned book so I went down there with my mate Big Dave – a tall and handsome guy who all the girls loved – to buy some of the copies with the intention of selling them on.

On the way back on the bus I had a eureka moment. Instead of trying to sell them, why not rent them for 25% of the selling price for a week so that by the fifth week we'd made all our money back, everything else was pure profit and we still had the books. If the school kids didn't pay up we'd send Big Daft Dave round to collect the debt for us and let him read the book for free as an added bonus.

Genius. We couldn't wait to put our plan into action so stopped off at St Patrick's Catholic School and shifted a few copies straightaway.

So we didn't just rent to the kids in our school. As natural-born entrepreneurs we thought big and rented them out to pupils at a few nearby schools too. Well, the wider your customer base, the more you'll make. Simple economics.

All went well for several months and we were coining it in but then we were suddenly summoned to the headmaster's office just before assembly one morning.

As soon as we walked in Mr Reid looked long and hard at us and then produced a copy of *Lady Chatterley's Lover*. He came straight to the point.

"Have either of you been selling this book to other schools in the area?" he asked. "Namely the Catholic school, Kirby Girls Grammar and Acklam Boys Grammar."

My response was quick, firm and honest.

"No, sir," I exclaimed.

"And you, David?" as Mr Reid turned to my partner in crime.

"Er, no sir," he said, sounding rather less convincing than me.

"Well," Mr Reid continued. "Can either of you tell me why three headmasters at three different schools in Middlesbrough are telling me that two boys wearing our school uniforms and answering to the names Graham and Dave are selling this book to their pupils?"

The game was up, but I wasn't giving in without a fight.

"We're not selling them, sir," I explained. "We're only renting them. Actually, we're already into profit and have more on order. Business is really booming."

Mr Reid held his hand up to stop my rambling.

"Leslie, you're totally missing the point," he said and launched into a full lecture on morality, refusing to listen to my argument that we'd done really well representing our school in such an enterprising way.

Minutes later we were duly punished, this time being caned in front of the whole school again. I was stripped of my roles as head boy and prefect and, even worse, told to hand over all my copies of *Lady Chatterley's Lover*.

As it turned out, I reckon all the action people wanted to read about in the book was on just one page so we'd done well to rake so much in and, actually, felt we'd done our bit for society by encouraging our peers to read so avidly at such a young age.

So that effectively ended my interest in school – today they'd call it 'engagement'.

Several years later I spoke to Mr Reid and asked him why he ever gave me such responsible roles. He said he saw me as a rebel but explained he was then faced with a choice to either try to break my spirit – which he felt was wrong as I was popular with other pupils – or give me some responsibility and hoped I'd mature into it. He was a very wise man although, in hindsight, I suppose I must have matured a bit late or I'd have still been in the roles on my last day there.

By the summer of 1962 I was getting school demob happy and was preparing to change the world by playing for the Middlesbrough boys' football team, competing for Yorkshire at athletics and was the Boys' Brigade champion for some sports and athletics for the north of England.

But a small group of us decided to leave our mark on Whinney

Banks on our final day.

Myself and a couple of co-conspirators, Derek Hill and Arthur Crosby – coincidentally all Leo birth signs if that means anything – hatched a plan to hang a pair of girl's knickers over the lightning conductor on the school tower.

The first problem was actually getting a pair as we knew no girls who would willingly part with their underwear so the only plan Derek and I could come up with was to nick a pair of knickers from a washing line.

Arthur, more a man of the world at the grand old age of 15, said "Leave it to me," duly disappeared and returned 30 minutes later with a pair. Even though it was 7pm I managed to get into the school and scaled the tower to attach the panties to the top where they fluttered magnificently in the breeze. It was no easy task, especially the last 12ft when I was holding onto nothing more substantial than mortar between the bricks.

Next morning was uproar with 350 pupils filing into assembly laughing and talking about the flying panties.

The humourless geography teacher Mr Gasgarth was walking behind me and used his walking stick to hook me round the neck and pulled me towards him.

He put his face close to mine and said "Leslie, do those belong to you?" as he pointed at the panties.

"No, sir," I replied. "They're not my size or colour."

And so ended my last day at school along with all the reports that kept on saying: "Graham could do so much better."

Heading for the catwalk ...
or possibly not

Having successfully failed my 11-plus exam I was labelled one of life's failures at school and left at 15 with, on paper, no qualifications.

I'd actually taken several subjects for the Northern Counties School Certificate but if you didn't have maths then you didn't get the certificate. I'd actually done well in English literature, geography, history, technical drawing, woodwork and religious education.

But maths and me didn't get on and without that no certificate was coming my way.

A few teachers had told me I was 'in a hurry to change the world' and the week before I left the careers teacher informed me that the computer age was on its way and I ought to go into a career that couldn't be automated so I'd have a job for life. Ahead of his years, really, that bloke.

I had a few careers in mind – professional footballer, rock star or racing driver – but always liked drawing and had noticed at the bottom right-hand corner of my dad's *Daily Telegraph* there was always a drawing of a beautiful lady wearing very elegant, fitted clothes, dresses or even suits to promote the famous brands of the day.

I also read a little about Mariano Fortuny, a Spaniard who moved to Italy and, with the help of his wife, Henriette Negrin, became one of the greatest ever dress designers.

Fortuny – what a brilliant name – was a great inspiration as his high fashions were worn by the best-known women of the age. So that was it, decision made. I was going to become a dress designer and change the fashion world.

I used some of my sister's eyeliner to pencil in what looked like the start of a moustache on my top lip to make me look older than I was and applied to become a student dress designer at Green Lane College of Art in Middlesbrough even though I was a year underage to enrol.

I was accepted onto the course starting in September and it got off to a very promising start on the second day when I was confronted by two nude ladies in the classroom and asked to sketch their voluptuous shapes.

I'd never seen a nude woman before or even a nude picture, let alone have to draw one. Yes, this dress design business was definitely for me, especially when I met up with friends at Rea's Café later – friends who had started work in the steelworks, with ICI or down the pit. They were slogging their guts out in often filthy workplaces while I was busy sketching nude women and not one, but two.

Fair to say I was asked a lot of probing questions about the female anatomy that I couldn't answer.

All I could say to get out of it was: "I was too busy drawing."

But it turns out fashion design isn't always about women and a few weeks later we were presented with two very well-equipped men in their 30s with honed torsos and the exuberance of the male students instantly evaporated to be replaced by excitement among the female ones.

I opted not to mention the male models in Rea's café, definitely a wise move to avoid public humiliation on the grandest of scales.

But all was not well in the Leslie world of dress design. A lecturer came up to me at the end of the first term and said: "Graham, can I have a word?"

Whenever someone says that it's always going to be more than a word and usually involves a problem. It certainly was as he showed me my sketching left a lot to be desired compared to work done by other students which was way better. It seemed that what was in my mind when I started to sketch and what actually ended up on the paper had some, well, let's just say disconnection.

The lecturer tried to be as kind as he could after seeing my hopes crumbling before him by adding: "Actually, Graham, your work reminds me a little bit of Henri de Toulouse-Lautrec."

When I answered in my complete ignorance, "Does he still play left back for Manchester United?" it rapidly became clear my six-week flirtation with dress design had come to an ignominious end.

I left that evening in October 1962 never to return to the college. But, on the upside, I then made it my mission to learn everything I could about Henri de Toulouse-Lautrec, which sparked my fascination with artists and how they can create such beauty at arm's length which is in full proportion when you view it at 20ft or so.

I knew I'd never be an artist but I also knew I'd always admire them for their skill, imagination, flair and vision, starting from a blank sheet of paper and going on to create something so eye-catchingly incredible.

When one door closes – in this case the art college one slammed in my face – another one usually opens.

Goodbye Graham ... hello André

The door that opened happened to be one in a hair salon.

My dad had his hair cut by Benny Lloyd who ran the top hairdressing salon in the North East and mentioned I was looking for a job so he agreed to interview me.

I passed it which earned me a sweeping brush and I spent the next few months clearing up the floor and cleaning the combs and brushes. You had to start at the bottom and, boy, was I on the bottom rung.

But my mum and dad paid a £100 bond, a cash sum to make sure I stuck to the three-year apprenticeship with Benny and I signed on as an Indentured Apprentice with the ultimate aim of achieving a City and Guilds qualification in haute de coiffure – that's the fancy French term for hair-styling – and I also learned wig-making.

The £100 was a lot in those days, especially as my dad's annual salary was only around £1,200 but it was worth every penny.

My first pay packet contained one pound, 17 shillings and 6p. I gave my mum the 17 shillings and sixpence towards housekeeping and I was left with a pound to live off for the next week.

Benny promised to teach and train me so I did the full three years even though I still secretly yearned for a career in singing or football and early on in my hairdressing years joined a rock group called The Defenders to try to earn some more money. I was lead singer doing impersonations of Elvis, Buddy Holly, Cliff Richard, Adam Faith and, er, Eartha Kitt.

We did a 'tour' of three working men's clubs plus Kirklevington Country Club near Yarm where we were asked back twice ... not to play but to be there in case the band they'd actually booked for those nights didn't turn up.

I think they also held my Eartha Kitt impression in reserve too in case they wanted to clear the place at the end of the night and go home early themselves.

Working with Benny Lloyd was far more than just hairdressing, it gave me an insight into market and upselling.

I realised just how important women's hair is to them ... it has to be just right. They must leave the salon feeling a million dollars or they'd be miserable, believing they look awful. Ladies can buy as many dresses, shoes and handbags as they want, but if their hair isn't right, then everything else doesn't count.

We were the first in the 1950s and 60s to bring in blow waving and styling and even started to colour and tint men's hair even though some worked down the pit or in the steelworks. They wanted to look great for the weekend and the upselling there was mainly condoms. As they paid they'd whisper 'can I have a packet of Johnnies or Good News' which we always gave them in a little plain brown bag. I earned my first commission selling them so I started to flog them around the rest of Middlesbrough too.

Benny was always after publicity for his salon and so encouraged us to enter hairdressing competitions. I'd been in a few which really boosted my confidence and won the British championship in Newcastle in the mid-1960s.

Benny saw my success as a marketing opportunity and decided I needed an image change to go 'upmarket'.

My middle name is Andrew and he thought my first name Graham a tad boring so he decided that from then on I'd be called André. He thought the name would mean my women clients would trust me even more and it made me sound flamboyant. My limited French did rather restrict the authenticity of my performance and I ended up just speaking English in a ridiculous French accent like the policeman out of *Allo Allo*. I also tried to sing to them in the style of Charles Aznavour and Maurice Chevalier.

My humiliation was complete in terms of the ribbing I got from my friends and girlfriends who then began to think I was gay. It took some convincing to prove to them I wasn't.

Another memorable hairdressing competition was in Blackpool where I tried my best to be Mr Flamboyant, walking to the stage to do my hairstyling spot in psychedelic flares to the sound of The Jackson 5 singing 'I Want You Back'. My showstopper routine was to do ringlets in three minutes and my secret weapon to achieve this was a setting lotion product called Glossone.

I'd crunch the dry hair back in a bunch and hold it in place with an elastic band. Then I'd set it in jumbo rollers on each side of the head and spray the Glossone on, blow-dry with hot air, take the rollers out and then pull the hair down into ringlets, add hairspray and it would set like rock.

It was a hectic time. I was working six days a week in the salon and on one evening a week teaching 20 young women studying their City and Guilds hairdressing at the new Stockton and Billingham Technical

College how to make wigs.

The wigs were made from real hair – sometimes from convents after women had cut off all their hair while becoming nuns – and had to be sewn into a mesh framework using watch springs. The critical parts were around the temples and nape of the neck to make sure it fitted properly.

More bizarrely, Benny won the contract to cut dead people's hair at the local Co-op funeral parlours two evenings a month. I only went once with Benny as I insisted on chatting to the deceased 'customers' as though they were still alive and it really unnerved him.

Benny was a real pioneer so also took his services out to people's homes and one was with the Rea family who had two brothers living next door to one another in Brookfield Gardens in what I can only describe as the biggest semi-detached house in Middlesbrough. The bathroom in one of them was larger than Benny's salon.

One of the Rea sons was called Chris who would be 12 or 13 then. Little did we know as we snipped away at his hair that he'd become one of the world's best-known singers. When Chris Rea is 'Driving Home for Christmas', he's heading back to Middlesbrough.

The family earned their money from running a very successful ice-cream business with several coffee bars and ice-cream parlours in Middlesbrough and places like Redcar and Guisborough. I certainly recall one at the entrance to Albert Park in Middlesbrough.

Benny also had links with a nightclub called Club Marimba and the stars performing there would come into the salon for a haircut or 'tidy up'.

Comedian Bob Monkhouse had us in stitches just talking as he was just so naturally funny and Lulu, who was then a teenager starting out, popped in with her mum. I met her again 45 years later when she performed at the Galpharm Stadium with Elton John in June 2005 and we chatted for ages about those days back in the 1960s. She's only small, but she's so much energy and what a voice with the personality to match.

One day Benny asked me if I'd do a hairdressing job in a hotel on my way home. So I went there, knocked on the door and it was opened by Dusty Springfield, a star at the time. I couldn't believe it, especially as she was also so famous for her blonde, bouffant, beehive hair. That sure tested my skills and nerves as an 18-year-old back combing and recreating that beehive.

It was the swinging 60s in every sense of the word – clothes, music, hair, everything – and I was keen to join this social revolution.

And so it was in 1964 I fell hopelessly in love with a very attractive natural blonde called Sandra Swale, a very successful hairdresser who was also on my college course one day a week.

Sandra also did some modelling and I was asked to model with her at a country club. Naturally I jumped at the chance. Here I was in the heart of the swinging 60s up on the catwalk.

It was all going great until I arrived at the venue to only then discover exactly what I was modelling. It was underpants. Yes, me in only some undies up in lights on the catwalk with loads of people gawping at me and my bits.

I managed to perform, if that's the right word, and left the catwalk, vowing never to return to modelling again.

Life was good with Sandra – happy teenage years of romance – until Sandra's father announced he had a new job for Rediffusion TV repair and rental. The problem was, the job was in Mansfield and so Sandra, who was 18 at the time, went with them.

It didn't stop me though and every weekend I'd drive down in my battered old van to see her and stay at her parents' house in Mansfield. Sandra worked at Redken's salon in Mansfield and one Saturday she had news for me which would change my life.

It was a cold, wet, damp day when we met outside the doctor's surgery.

"I'm pregnant," she said.

"How?" I replied as, I suppose, any idiotic young man would and then followed it up with the even dumber: "Does that mean having a baby?"

"Yes, in six months," came her response which had soared in pitch to a kind of scream as her initial calm approach had descended quickly into the reality of what we both now faced.

Sandra added: "We need to tell my mum and dad and then you need to drive back to Middlesbrough and tell your mum and dad, leave your pals and work and get down here and get a job so we can set up home together. Mum and Dad won't want you in their home."

So I drove home worried about how my parents would react. After all, they were strictly religious and both highly respected in the church, the community and the town. How could I possibly limit the damage of what I was about to tell them?

My parents were sitting in the small kitchen at our home on Malvern Drive when I told them the shattering news. That led to a long and very difficult discussion with Mum being very understanding and Dad the exact opposite with the talk veering from me leaving or the baby being adopted or even an abortion.

Dad felt I'd brought a huge disgrace on my family. He was a man of great integrity and morals and the swinging 60s were totally alien to him.

I insisted I loved Sandra and would leave home and Middlesbrough, family and friends, move to Mansfield to be with her and get married.

Dad drove me to the edge of the Yorkshire border with the A1 and then told me to get out and thumb a lift to Mansfield.

So that's just what I did, arriving in Mansfield with just £28 in my pocket, the clothes on my back and my football kit in a rucksack.

Settling down with Sandra

My first job was driving ... an electric vehicle.

It would be great to say I was 50 years ahead of my time but it was actually a battery-driven Co-Op delivery cart dropping bread off at miners' homes in Bildworth and Rainworth. When the battery went flat you just didn't get home until around 9pm.

This usually happened on the way back to the depot so you'd have to go and find a phone box, give them a call and they'd tow you back to the charging points in the compound shed. I used to deliver to a lot of the villages around Mansfield so I often fell 10 miles short with my battery power. People with electric cars still have the same problems today – it's called range anxiety now – but just on a different scale as they could be hundreds of miles from home frantically searching for a charging point.

I also had a one-night job ... as a bouncer. It was at the local cinema where they were showing the James Bond classic *Goldfinger* and I heard a lot of moaning and groaning on the back seat so, naturally, I flicked my torch on and shone it to see what was going on.

I was greeted with the memorable words: "If you don't switch that bloody torch off I'll stick it up you're a***."

Not wishing to suffer the indignity and, probably considerable pain and embarrassment of having a torch shoved where the sun doesn't shine, I switched it off and never went back to the job.

Sandra managed to get me an interview with a hairdressing wholesalers on Market Street in Mansfield called A J Bells. I passed thanks to my hairdressing background and within a week had a job and a van.

I had to find my own digs and that was a bizarre experience that almost ended our relationship.

I managed to get an attic room on Baums Lane in Mansfield and there were several girls in the rooms below who told me they were nurses at the local hospital working shifts. Several evenings a week they would come up to my room late at night, around 11pm, usually in their underwear and a T-shirt to drink, play cards and chat. I'd sometimes do their hair and, in return, they'd iron me a shirt or two.

We were great pals and then one evening the police raided the building and we were escorted out into the street. The local paper must have been tipped off as the next day there was a photo on the front page showing me walking down the stairs with the ladies. It turned out I was living at the top of a brothel.

I'm sure half the street knew what was going on but, it seems, I was the last to know. Even the police realised I was hopelessly naïve so they didn't actually arrest me and take me to the police station.

Sandra's mother, Alice, didn't take the news well and ended up frothing at the mouth in anger, saying she never wanted to see me again.

Anyhow, that wish went ungranted as Sandra and I married on April 10, 1967 at the Methodist church in Mansfield Woodhouse. Sandra always insisted that I married her for her money. I had just £28 while she had £58. Our son, Craig, was born four months later on August 22. I saw him as my 21st birthday present.

We bought our first home on the aptly-named Crookes Avenue and the number was 14. It was aptly named as we were certainly conned with the valuation. The woman selling the house basically owned the street and said we could use her solicitor to save money and we were assured the valuation, £1,450, was correct. She then actually loaned us the money for the mortgage so we paid her every month. When we moved to Huddersfield in 1971 she insisted on buying the house from us but paid £100 less than what we had bought it for. Turns out she'd inflated the value when she originally sold it to us and we'd fallen for it. We were conned.

It was now around 1968 and we had very little money so Sandra took her first engagement ring to the pawnbrokers so she could treat us to some fillet steaks from the local butcher at the end of the street.

A couple of days later we found her dog Bran, a cream Alsatian, trying to get a side of lamb into his kennel at our back door which he must have grabbed from a nearby abattoir. Times were hard so Sandra cooked it up and we all shared it, including Bran for getting it in the first place.

But life was improving and I won a trip to New York as a prize for selling lots of Clairol hair products. I remember shopping at Macy's on Fifth Avenue, visiting Fred Astaire's dance studio on Manhattan Island and bringing Craig home a little yellow zipper jacket with a turtle on. He'd have been three then and I was in my mid-20s.

It also put me in the limelight in the hair product sales world and I ended up being headhunted (yes, that pun was intended) by Don Fisher from Schwarzkopf as he heard I'd been British champion hairdresser and then achieved top sales for Clairol.

My life had changed again in another way too as our daughter, Amanda, was born on May 14, 1969.

Schwarzkopf was a turning point in my work life as it gave me the chance to understand brand marketing, to travel and demonstrate the products and it also meant I could have a company car.

I was on my way.

Hello Huddersfield

The year 1971 marked another career turning point as Sandra's dad had been offered a new job in the Rediffusion head office in Bradford so they moved to Brighouse.

We followed as by now I was travelling all over the Midlands and the north so we decided to move to Huddersfield and our first home was on the Bankfield Park Avenue estate at Taylor Hill. It cost £2,400, was a new build by well-known Huddersfield company Jack Brook (Builders) Ltd and was full of comers-in ... like me.

I had a large Ford Zephyr Zodiac estate with the Schwarzkopf logo emblazoned down the sides and, bizarrely, my competitors were my neighbours with the sales rep for *L'Oréal* living next door and the Wella rep a few doors further down.

There was a terribly sad story behind the land where the Bankfield estate was built. It was a mill owner's stately home but the business had gone to the wall after a load of cloth destined for export had got caught up in a dockers' strike in Liverpool and two of the family members connected with the business then took their own lives.

The pressures on business owners are always immense and way too many end in tragedy when it becomes all too much. Thankfully there's more awareness about mental health these days, especially men's mental health. I only hope that people can now get the help they need when they feel they have nowhere else to turn.

The land at Bankfield Park was sold and the builders got permission to build 50 homes on it. We needed a garage but had no money to get someone to do it so I ended up building it myself.

My dad had given us £100 and Sandra used it to set up her first hair salon in the village of Thrybergh in Rotherham. She would drive over in her second-hand Mini van every day and take the children with her during school holidays. It didn't have enough power to get up to 60mph and had a leaky battery in the back which Craig used to sit on and he sometimes ended up with acid burns. That's the 70s for you. Health and safety hadn't been 'invented' by then.

My first sales course at Schwarzkopf was led by a guy called Jim Mollison from Lancashire who taught me the art of 'optional selling'.

He did it with the launch of a new dispenser for the Glossone setting lotion. He'd show clients the product, spray it on his hands to prove how beautifully scented it was and then tell them that as a trial they could have 14 to the dozen or 12 and two free. Most chose the 12 and two free but he was the top salesman in the company by volume and value in what was the poorest demographic area in the country.

I discovered the only way in those days to legitimately avoid paying capital gains tax was to move house as often as you could. If it was your home and you made a profit on it then you didn't have to pay any tax on that gain.

So we looked at purchasing property and I bought a terraced house in Moldgreen which I had to live in for a while to avoid paying the tax on it.

But my strangest property buying experience was yet to come. I went to an auction – my first ever – and started to bid for a property on Lockwood Road in Huddersfield. My lucky ticket number was 27 and in no time at all I was the highest bidder for the house at £1,800.

I ambled over to the solicitor's table to sign for it when I was given three documents to sign and told I'd bought three properties. I was flabbergasted and shocked. I only had enough to buy one and my first thought was I'd bought three for £1,800 each, making it a grand total of £5,400 – money I simply didn't have.

I apologised profusely and said I thought I was bidding for just one property for £1,800 but was told I'd actually bought all three for £1,800. I was so relieved and went on to make a very nice profit from that error.

While we were developing the three properties I asked my insurance broker to insure the derelict houses. He told me not to bother as there was nothing worth stealing, but when I drove past the following week I discovered that thieves had stolen the grey stone slates off the roofs.

So that was my first lesson on insurance. Never under insure.

In life when you think things are running fine suddenly something jumps up to kick you in the teeth.

I'd been made a 'Schwarzkopf Knight' for being a top salesman for a few years and demonstrated the company's products at the Blackpool International Hair Show so they invited me to go for an interview at the company's head office in Aylesbury for the job of national sales director.

I jumped at the chance and drove down in my Hillman Avenger – the one with the go faster stripes – to Buckinghamshire for what I thought was the chance of a lifetime. During the interview the company managing director asked me if I could work with a guy from the south of England if he was made sales director instead of me.

I thought he wanted an honest answer so I gave him one. I knew the bloke and urged the managing director not to promote him as the team had no respect for him and he wasn't in the best of health anyway.

I left the interview feeling I'd done myself proud and waited in reception with the only other candidate, Trevor from Sheffield.

Twenty minutes later the boss came into reception and dropped the bombshell that he was appointing the guy from the south.

But that wasn't all. He told us we were both leaving the company with immediate effect and to leave our car keys and all our records in the office and get the train back home.

Shocked, I looked at Trevor and he looked at me.

Then Trevor said: "I'm leaving my car in reception, not just the keys."

I could see by the whites of his eyes that he wasn't joking so as he walked out to rev up his car I grabbed the young receptionist from behind the counter and led her out into the car park and safety.

Trevor then drove his Avenger straight into the glass reception area before calmly walking out and catching the train with me. The only time we spoke on the journey was to say 'cheerio' and I never saw him again.

As for the successful candidate, he lasted a year in the job and then retired due to ill health.

Life on the dole ...
but things can only get better

Life had suddenly become challenging.

In the spring of 1972 I was, how they say, 'in between jobs', with a huge mortgage and young family but no income so we were relying on Sandra's hair salon to survive.

By this time she had moved from Rotherham to Holmfirth where her salon called Pratty Hair – after the Holmfirth anthem Pratty Flowers – was opposite the art gallery owned by a man who was to become a global brand synonymous with the Holme Valley. That was Ashley Jackson and his paintings of the moors around Huddersfield are phenomenal. An artist who actually makes money ... now that's unusual in itself. Artists are so incredibly talented yet making money can be very tough for them.

With no job on the immediate horizon I went to the dole office in a grim red-brick building on Queen Street South in Huddersfield with Amanda who was around two years old in the pushchair and holding Craig by the hand.

It was a miserable, thoroughly demoralising experience worsened by my own honesty.

They asked me how much I had in savings and I told them the truth – £312 – so they told me I'd need to live off all my savings first and when they were gone to come back to sign on.

By this time Amanda was shrieking and Craig was, to say the least, restless, as I battled with the officials to try to make them see sense. I'd done the right thing by putting savings aside but it seemed to be the wrong thing to do now I was in a position where I'd needed to rely on the State for the first time in my working life.

Frustrated, I tried in vain to argue my case but the official was having none of it and the next minute I felt an arm around my shoulders. I looked round to see a Rastafarian guy gently leading me away from the counter to some seats, urging me to calm down.

I'll always remember what he said to me: "The only thing you did wrong, man, was to tell the truth."

I'll never forget his kindness and compassion.

As it was, a man and a woman from the dole office came round to our house to do a means test and were genuinely shocked to discover we couldn't afford a carpet – we'd painted the pine floorboards green – or a settee. We just had big cushions spread around the floor and, bizarrely, a hanging basket in the corner. Well, it was the early 1970s so I suppose that basket was my Hare Krishna Beatles-style moment.

The garishness was ramped up another notch when they spotted we'd painted the kitchen red. They were so sure we must have hidden our furniture somewhere they went round to a neighbour's to check it wasn't stored there.

In the end I never got a penny from the dole and learned a harsh lesson about the perils of honesty and wondered why people bothered to work hard and save in the first place.

So I had to think differently to make some money and this is where it all turns into the kind of comedy episode you'd see on *Only Fools and Horses* with me in the Del Boy Trotter role.

I knew how to make shampoo – of a fashion – and mixed huge batches in the bath using a base soap, liquid, colour and salt to thicken it up. I'd bought a few one-gallon containers but then pondered how to get it out of the bath and into the containers.

Then I had a brainwave. I pulled the plug on the bath, sprinted outside with the one-gallon plastic containers and caught it as it slithered down the drainpipe, but quite a lot still escaped onto our patio.

I called it Pearlised shampoo and it came in two colours – pink for female salons and blue for male. Then it was a case of getting on my bike and riding as far as Brighouse to flog it to as many local hairdressers as I could. As it was cheap, delivered free and the salons weren't bothered about the somewhat basic packaging, many bought it and I'd soon built up quite a round, although I'm not sure my homemade concoction was that good for their clients' hair. Still, it was the 70s and anything seemed to go then.

Anyway, all was going well until there was a heavy thunderstorm overnight and the torrential rain washed all the shampoo left on the patio into the street, turning our garden and half the road into a giant bubble bath.

Still, it was a talking point for the neighbours. Another tip from that time was to always get to know your neighbours as you never know when you might need their help.

I'd hoarded around 60 bottles of wine stacked in the garage left over from a Schwarzkopf promotion so had the idea for an impromptu street party, invited all the neighbours and we spent a great afternoon getting sozzled.

That party turned out to be the catalyst for my most life-changing moment.

I'd applied for 30 sales jobs but only got a couple of interviews. I was rejected from one after the interview panel asked me what annoyed me most and I replied: "People who don't indicate while driving."

That seemed to irritate them for some reason. Perhaps they were habitual non-indicators.

But then an interview chance popped up for a job at Winthrop Pharmaceuticals in York. The problem was I didn't have a car but a neighbour who had been to the street party then offered to drive me all the way there in her yellow VW Beetle.

It changed my life completely. If she hadn't been kind enough to give me a lift that day my life would have been totally different. I was at a massive crossroads in life – even though I didn't know it at the time – and she took me the right way.

I was interviewed by the wonderfully-named Tony Hope and Dennis Corson from Winthrop – two men who were to play such a crucial role that set me on the way to founding my own multi-million-pound pharmaceutical company. I still call Dennis 'the Boss' as he was the Brian Clough of the pharmaceutical industry at that time, successfully launching several medicines, such as Panadol, which became household brands.

They interviewed me for an hour and offered me the job there and then, although Tony later confided he'd decided he wanted me to work for him after just 30 seconds.

At that point pharmaceutical companies only employed would-be doctors or chemists who had never actually finished their exams or failed to qualify to sell their medicines to pharmacies and promote them to GP practices so they'd appear on prescriptions.

But Tony saw something in me. He didn't need someone with medical knowledge. He needed someone who could sell and I'll be forever grateful for the chance he gave me.

They took a punt on me as their first non-academic medical representative and then gave me all the support in the world when even I lost faith in myself.

I remember on the drive back home I thought, 'How the hell am I going to do this. I know nothing about medicines."

How my pharmaceutical career was almost over before it began

So I was sent on a training course to Surbiton in southwest London and that's when I realised I had a major problem. The trainers were talking about the chemical formula for the drugs and I realised I couldn't read the generic drug names, pronounce them or, more importantly, spell them. What was wrong with me?

One of the women on the course from the Winthrop head office tried to help me and one day she was reading a book. I looked over her shoulder, pointed to a word and asked her what it said. She told me it was a word I used all the time so why couldn't I read it? The word was 'hypothetical' and at that moment in my late 20s the penny finally dropped. I realised I was dyslexic and that's the reason I'd had so much trouble reading in my childhood and taken so many canings and beatings for it.

They'd thought I was naughty, lazy or cheeky. My mum was so upset when I finally revealed the diagnosis and she realised the punishments and tellings-off I'd gone through as a child were unjustified.

My eyes filled with tears as I feared that was it, my career in pharmaceuticals was over even before it had begun.

I called Tony, told him I was sure I was dyslexic so couldn't do the course and that I was resigning.

But, God bless him, Tony made it clear his faith in me remained as strong as ever and told me: "You're my test case to prove that successful sales and marketing people can become successful medical sales people. You're not going to fail and we'll get you through this."

We got around it by me talking to the customers and then seeking help from colleagues when anything needed writing down. It also started me thinking about what I could have made of myself if I'd been able to read properly.

If Tony hadn't had that absolute faith in me all those years ago then I'd have walked away from pharmaceuticals and Galpharm would never have happened.

Tony was a visionary and with me as a natural salesman – albeit one that shunned writing wherever possible – I was determined to do all I could to make it work, so much so I was named the company's

Man of the Year not long after, which shows that the industry was totally male-dominated. In the mid-70s Winthrop appointed a female sales rep – I think she was the first one in the country – and the title was changed to Representative of the Year.

In the 1970s many medicines could only be acquired through a visit to the doctor to get them prescribed. Tony's role as sales director was to cut out the GP visits as most were completely unnecessary and sell them direct to pharmacies, so-called over the counter.

This was a completely new concept in the UK at the time and it was a win-win. Although the chemists were paid for every prescription they dispensed, what they'd lose on not having the prescriptions anymore they'd easily make up from the profits on the direct sales to customers. It would also save GPs wasted time writing out prescriptions they didn't really need to do.

The three medicines we started with were Panadol for headaches, pain and fevers; Selenium for dandruff and Actal antacid for indigestion. We'd take time to talk to the chemist counter assistants, hoping they'd then recommend them to customers, and Actal was an especially good one as it was one of very few antacids safe for pregnant women to take with many of them suffering from heartburn and indigestion.

In those early days, as now really, I was always coming up with ideas. When Winthrop produced a Panadol Elixir for children I suggested promoting it heavily in GP surgeries and health centres and wanted district nurses to carry it around so they always had a bottle for patients. If a doctor or nurse suggests a medicine by name there's no more powerful form of natural brand promotion.

I'd try to get round 12 pharmacies a day – 60 in a week – and we all had 'Doctor On Call' cards for cars to give away to doctors with the Winthrop name on the back so the GPs would see our name every day when they were out and about visiting patients.

Obviously the temptation proved too much and some of the sales reps started to use the cards themselves – after all, we had thousands of pounds of medicines in the boot so didn't want to let the car out of sight, which is why most rep cars ended up on double yellow lines outside pharmacies. Sometimes we had medicines worth up to £5,000 in the boot which was nearly the equivalent of my annual salary.

My car especially stood out as by that stage it was a red Avenger with go faster stripes down the side and a fairing on the back. Don't judge me too harshly. I was young with a growing fascination for cars.

Protected from traffic wardens by our cheeky cards, we could park anywhere and no-one would question it but, like all these slightly dodgy ideas, you'll eventually get caught out.

I came a cropper when I parked far too near to Elland Road while Leeds United were playing at home with the 'Doctor On Call' card still in the window.

As we were leaving there was a right punch-up going on with one lad covered in blood after he'd been headbutted. His mate, a massive bloke, ran over to my car, banged on the window and then unceremoniously dragged me out, urging me to go and help as I was a doctor. I mumbled some lame excuse about it being my brother's car and drove away. I never misused that card again. Some lessons you learn the hard way.

Another 'bad day at the office' happened when I was parked in Rotherham and when I came out of the pharmacy I noticed the front of my car was all bashed in. There was a bus queue nearby so I asked if anyone had seen what had happened. A man said he had but it was OK as the offending driver who had smashed into my car had left a note under my windscreen wiper.

That was a relief as at least I'd have his insurance details, but my heart sank like the proverbial stone when I read it. It said: "Everyone thinks I'm leaving my details but I'm not. Tough shit."

The day Sir Stanley Matthews ran rings round me

I also had some great times at Winthrop although many bordered on the bizarre.

We were at a conference in Valletta, the capital of Malta, when someone suggested a game of football between the hotel guests and the local post office team. We turned up to a bone-hard clay pitch with the tiniest bits of grass left on it, but ended up staring at one of the opposition players.

He seemed so familiar even though he'd have been around 60. Then it dawned on me – he was legendary English footballer Sir Stanley Matthews who played professionally from 1932 until he retired in 1965 aged 50 and, of course, starred in the 1953 FA Cup Final where he created three goals in the second half to turn what looked like a 3–1 defeat to Bolton into a 4–3 victory for Blackpool.

Turns out he'd gone to live in Malta after he'd retired but we've still no idea how he ended up in the Malta post office team. He was, I guess, the ultimate ringer. We never got near him – he was utter class, literally dancing around us and we watched him in awe as we were hammered something like 7–2.

Another freakish thing happened to us when we were doing a sales training course in Tenerife and, hands up, I definitely brought this one on myself.

After gruelling days in the classroom we relaxed in the disco underneath the hotel and I came up with the idea to make us more interesting to the women. Instead of admitting we were sales reps, we claimed we were airline pilots to impress the ladies. It was working too until a group of actual Lufthansa pilots turned up and wanted to 'talk shop' with the British pilots. We made our excuses and hurriedly left.

After that close shave I thought it worth another go but this time, as we knew about medicines, we'd pretend to be doctors attending a global conference discussing anaesthetics. What could possibly go wrong?

Well, a lot, actually.

In the early hours of the morning there was a loud knock on my door. One of the reps rushed in with some garbled message about me being needed at the local hospital.

He said: "The woman I'm with said you are the only one she trusts to operate on her friend."

Within minutes company bosses were in my room along with other reps and their various female companions wanting to know what was going on.

Turns out one of my team had got rather carried away with the doctors yarn, pointed me out and claimed I was a top surgeon.

To make matters both ironic and worse it turns out this poor lady had taken an overdose of Winthrop analgesics so I was expected to go and pump her stomach out.

I'd run out of options so went to the hospital. The woman's friend had told the hospital the hotel was full of English doctors and she wanted one of us to perform the operation – me – as it looked like it could be a matter of life or death.

I arrived at the hospital with my entourage – almost like a consultant doing his rounds – to be greeted by the hospital's registrar. How on earth do I get out of this, I thought. So I told him his hospital had a brilliant reputation and I was more than happy to leave the operation to him and he was to carry on with my full support.

We got back to the hotel at around 3.30am and were up by 7am for our first conference meeting. About 8pm that evening the hotel tannoy announced that Dr Leslie was needed at reception.

Fearing the worst I went down wondering what could possibly happen next, to be greeted by the friend of the woman who had had her stomach pumped. She thanked me for all I'd done and said the operation had gone well.

I never did that role play thing again … well, not at a conference. If you pretend, it's likely to bite you on the backside … hard.

The Winthrop job was going well, so much so I was able to buy land and build my own house in Holmbridge in 1976 – the year of the great drought and standpipes. I'd always hoped to build my own home by the time I was 30 and I turned 30 that year. The total cost to build it, including the land, was £23,000.

By that time I was chairman and player at Wooldale Wanderers AFC, which held an annual fundraising event to raise money to keep the club solvent. It usually starred local comedian Ceddie Beaumont and a couple of girls who stripped off … and the more the audience paid, the more 'entertaining' they became.

Well, naturally, it was a sell-out every year but during one of the evenings the club secretary asked me to urgently go backstage as the girls were refusing to go back on stage unless they got more money. I had 250 excited men in the audience who had been on the booze so I didn't want to let them down.

I reached the dressing area to be confronted by two very scantily clad ladies and one who was completely naked who told me to sit down and then sat across me and strangled me. I looked her straight in the eyes, said we had an agreement and would she please stop throttling me, go back on stage and continue the show.

But she simply said: "You go out there and strip."

Feeling the lads in the crowd would be a tad disappointed with me appearing on stage stripping, I paid the girls what they wanted and left the dressing room as quickly as I possibly could.

The next morning, a Saturday, I was walking through Huddersfield with my mum when I was stopped by a very attractive young lady rattling a tin, asking if we'd like to make a donation to a children's charity.

My mum said: "Of course, dear. We'd love to and how wonderful of you to give up your time on a Saturday for such a good cause."

I looked at the young lady, smiled and winked as I popped our contribution into her tin.

She smiled back and said: "Thank you, sir. You look the generous sort."

It was the same lady who the night before had straddled me naked, negotiating her own terms as she choked me.

Mum added as we walked away: "What a lovely young lady. You should meet someone like that and settle down."

About this time a friend who was headteacher at a local school, Ian McKay, asked me to help as he was battling with Kirklees Council over the need for separate changing areas as one of his pupils was developing into an excellent footballer and cricketer.

We were successful and the pupil went on to represent England at both cricket and football, a first for women's sport in the north.

I've always been a supporter of women's football. In the late 1970s I was asked to train a ladies football team – one of the first in Huddersfield – which I did every Sunday at the Reinwood recreation ground at Oakes for a season. Huddersfield Town Women FC now play all their home games at the Leslie Sports Foundation site at Storthes Hall.

Ian became headteacher at another local school when the staff, led astray by a young lady student teacher, made him a chocolate cake for his birthday but laced it with laxative and he spent the next few days either on or very close to a toilet.

Ian wanted revenge so roped me in to playing the part of a school inspector and briefed me on exactly what he wanted me to do.

It was on the final day before the school broke up for the Christmas holiday and I reported to the reception, clipboard in hand and confidently claimed to be from the Yorkshire Schools Inspection Board, not that such an organisation actually exists.

I said the first teacher on my list to observe was the young student teacher and asked to be taken to her classroom.

I told her I was a school inspector and to pay no attention to me as I sat at the back of the classroom but would be grading her for the next stage in her career.

Afterwards, I asked to speak to her alone and then told her that today would be a career-changing one for her.

She asked how she'd done and I said she had excellent marks for her presentation skills to the students but there was a problem about how she conducted herself with colleagues and that giving a headteacher a cake laced with laxative was, well, detrimental to her career progression.

Her face dropped like a stone and then she actually broke down in tears, even though I softened and said it was just a joke. In the end I confessed that Ian had brought me in to get his own back and then he came into the room and said to her: "Got you."

Her reply is unprintable but it wasn't detrimental to her career.

Meanwhile, Winthrop sales were starting to boom and here's why.

On the side of all medicines you'll find one or more of these three symbols – POM, P or GSL. POM means prescription only, P means pharmacy only while GSL means it's on the General Sales List so can be sold in any retail outlets from pharmacies to corner shops, supermarkets and vending machines.

Thing is, many pharmaceutical companies only wanted to sell through prescription only or pharmacies as it gave them more control over keeping the prices high. Selling them through loads of retail outlets would inevitably trigger a price war and bring their profits down.

Getting medicines on the General Sales List was the business model that was to later drive Galpharm Pharmaceuticals to such incredible success.

By around 1977 I was beginning to feel strongly that medicines should be made cheaper for the mass of people and didn't like the way the big companies were protecting their markets and keeping prices so high.

I came up with a way for Winthrop to do this and still make around 80% profit, but was rejected because, as it turned out, they were making even bigger profits doing it their way.

So, customers were paying far too much for some medicines and I was also getting more and more worried about how much the NHS was having to spend for these medicines when I knew they could be sold far cheaper. I've no problem with companies making profits but they should be fair.

I'd served my apprenticeship and was ready to jump ship, but before I did my entrepreneurial spirit took over once more and my never-ending search for the 'thrill of the kill' kicked in. That's buying a product, selling the product on, making a profit and keeping the customer happy. That thrill never leaves me.

Winthrop was over-producing some medicines so I formed a company called PH Supplies and rented warehouse space in a mill off Dunford Road in Holmfirth.

I bought surplus stock – usually paracetamol – from Winthrop and sold it to cash and carry warehouses mainly in Manchester but also London, Birmingham and Leeds who then sold them to corner shops.

Someone told me vast profits were to be made selling mascara from the UK to China and Hong Kong, so I bought loads of mascara from a cash and carry in Manchester, found an agent in Kowloon in Hong Kong and Craig helped me to pack them up to send over there from Holmfirth post office. We probably made around 10 times our initial outlay.

The cash and carry places were for trade only and were an Aladdin's cave of ideas and I ended up buying pots and pans along with gold-plated cutlery, doubling the price and selling them through adverts in national newspapers.

As for the business name PH Supplies, it actually stood for Pratty Hair Supplies to coincide with Sandra's salon in Holmfirth.

You can't get more local than that yet here I was selling make-up to the other side of the world from a sideline in Holmfirth.

But, as it turned out, this was just the start of something far, far bigger.

Getting going with Galpharm

My sideline company PH Supplies was buying its stock of paracetamol, aspirin, soluble aspirin and saccharine sweeteners from medicines manufacturer Wallis Laboratory based in Luton and then selling it through the big cash and carry stores.

They were then selling it on to the small corner shops.

It meant that most weekends I was driving down to Luton in a van to pick my supplies up and then dropping them off at the cash and carry places the same weekend or during the evenings.

This worked well until 1982 when a chance meeting changed everything.

Wallis sales manager Peter Fisher had gone on holiday to Tenerife and by sheer chance one of my colleagues from Winthrop, Mike Mitchell, was staying in the same hotel and they got chatting at the bar.

When talk turned to pharmaceuticals Peter asked Mike if he'd heard of a Graham Leslie. Apparently Mike didn't let on he knew me to find out how Peter knew me and Peter then revealed that PH Supplies was one of Wallis's best customers and was supplying drug stores across the UK.

Mike didn't mention a word of this to me but as soon as he got back home went straight to Winthrop sales director Keith Hazelwood who summoned me to the Surbiton head office.

I knew something was wrong before I even set off. Usually we were provided with first-class train tickets. This time they were second class.

As soon as I arrived Keith got straight to the point and asked me what I knew about PH Supplies.

"Everything," I replied. "I set up and own the company and it's been going a while now."

Keith was furious, especially as he regarded the over-the-counter generic paracetamols I was getting from Wallis as a rival to the Panadol produced by Winthrop.

I had a safety net though as I'd told Winthrop I had a company called PH Supplies when I joined them but at that time it was concentrating on selling mascara to China.

I told Keith: "You can't sack me because I'd told you about this company and PH Supplies has been a convenient way for Winthrop to get rid of surplus stock which I bought from the company."

Keith wanted to sack me on the spot but then realised he couldn't. In the end he decided to wait for the Winthrop managing director to return from holiday to make a decision on my fate.

As it turned out he actually wanted me to stay. He was pushing the Winthrop brands in Europe and wanted me to join him doing that but I told him I'd enough struggles with the English language without trying to cope with French or German.

He was a lovely man and a pioneer and once, while we were on a business trip together, he said that the higher you go in a company, the more isolated and lonelier it gets.

"You don't trust anyone," he said. "But I trust you."

I went on holiday to Scotland to mull things over, made my decision and called him from a phone box on Oban to say I was leaving.

The wage at Winthrop wasn't huge – £8,700 a year back in 1982 – but the expenses were brilliant and ran into five-figure sums each year so I'd be leaving a decent living and taking a risk.

But it was the time to do it. I knew my journey with Winthrop had hit the buffers and was also surprised to learn during all the shenanigans that PH Supplies was responsible for 25% of the Wallis Laboratory sales. I never knew that until all this blew up.

It was time to start a new journey in the world of business, but I was short of cash to buy more stock and search for more products, not helped by the fact that I was going through a divorce.

So one Saturday morning I popped into the local branch of Lloyds Bank in Holmfirth – the town famous for its central role in long-running BBC TV sitcom *Last of the Summer Wine* – and spoke to the bank manager, Bob Riley.

He was in the local Round Table with me but I was far from confident he'd let me have the loan facility of up to £5,000 I was requesting.

I'd gone in low-key in jeans, wellies, a dark speckled brown polo neck jumper and … my guitar. That was pretty much all I had at the time apart from my 19ft-long sailing boat *Curlew* parked on a trailer outside hitched up to my green Ford Cortina.

He hit me with the question I knew was coming and was dreading.

"What collateral do you have Graham?" he asked.

He was met by silence so repeated the question.

"You're looking at my greatest assets," I eventually said. "Me and my guitar."

"Really?" he replied. "Well, go on then, play me a tune."

"I can't play it," I said. "I've just brought it along for company."

He laughed, backed his judgement by giving me the loan, but I only ever used £4,000 of it which really helped to accelerate the business and the rest was all paid back on time. He'd backed the right jockey.

I also needed an accountant and a solicitor. My accountant became Melvyn Hoyle from Holmfirth accountants Rogers and Co and Paul Brown from Heap, Marshall and Heeley became the company's solicitor. Both great men who were vital to Galpharm's ultimate success and shows the importance of having a strong, loyal team around you that you can trust.

Next job, a new name for the company. Up to then we'd been what's known as opportunist traders but I decided it was now time to concentrate on pharmaceuticals. To be blunt, I needed a name that made the business sound bigger than it was and so wanted pharmaceuticals – or at least pharm – in it. Any name had to be registered with the Pharmaceutical Society or it would be illegal to trade in the industry.

I suggested Worldpharm, Britpharm and even Europharm but they turned me down every time saying we weren't a large enough company to justify such a name. On the seventh attempt and in sheer frustration I came up with Galpharm – which are my initials for Graham Andrew Leslie with Pharm stuck on the end. They tried to reject that too but I said they couldn't really as it was my initials so they let this one go. It was a great result in the end as Galpharm kind of trips off the tongue and is a name people tend to remember.

We then looked for larger premises in Huddersfield. We were outgrowing our space in the mill on Dunford Road in Holmfirth but mill owner Selwyn Smith had been brilliant with us, letting us have it for a peppercorn rent.

Selwyn was an entrepreneur who refurbished old mill equipment and then exported them all over the world ... but he ended up branching out into natural spring water and this is how it's supposed to have happened.

They were unloading a machine at their mill yard in Shepley when it fell and smashed the cobbles. They then noticed water coming out and tried to fix the problem with concrete but the water simply wouldn't stop bubbling up. They investigated further, discovered it was a natural spring and so they came up with the idea for Shepley Spring bottled water and it's now the largest family-owned bottled water manufacturer in the UK selling to huge supermarkets such as

Sainsbury's, Tesco, Lidl and Morrisons.

We left Holmfirth and moved to N Battye Mills – known locally as Aspley Mills – on Firth Street next to Huddersfield town centre. The mill is now demolished and replaced by student accommodation and the 3M Buckley Innovation Centre which became so important in my life decades later.

We had a 1,500-square-foot, single-storey unit round the back of the mill with an office next to the road. It's close to the River Colne so we had a problem with water rats sneaking in and stealing any crisps we left lying around. In the end we had to put traps in the warehouse when they started to gnaw on the bars of soap we stocked there.

Money was tight but salvation came even though I managed to negotiate myself out of £5,000 a year. Wallis Laboratory owner Paul Deverell was upset at what had happened with Winthrop so he offered me money to work as a consultant for him.

He offered me £15,000 a year and, as I'd been earning just under £9,000 at Winthrop, I couldn't believe I'd be earning so much more as a consultant.

"How much?" I replied.

Paul said: "Well, if that's not enough how about £20,000?"

"No, no," I said. "£15,000 is fine."

And that's how I talked myself out of £5,000 in a couple of seconds.

It did mean Paul always got objective, no-nonsense advice from me and when he came under pressure within the company to diversify and go into vitamins I advised him strongly against it and to concentrate on what they did best ... pharmaceuticals.

Galpharm's first chairman was my dad, Hugh, but, very sadly, his tenure was all-too-short and he died in 1983.

He'd left his mark on the Probation Service. When he was in Middlesbrough he set up a hostel for ex-prisoners against vociferous protests from local people.

Rather than just impose the plan, he organised public meetings and faced his critics head-on, telling them: "These people are coming out of prison anyway and they could be living next door to you and you wouldn't know it. By having a hostel we know where they'll be, you know where they'll be and we'll be helping to reintegrate them into society."

He was a pioneer who knew the value of public relations and headed it up himself, never shirking from his decisions or responsibilities and had a real sense of openness, telling people just how it was.

When he retired as principal probation officer for Teesside he and my mum, Anne, moved to Scotland and lived in the town of Largs on the Firth of Clyde where they had done their courting in the 1930s.

Dad knew he'd had a slight stroke but didn't tell anyone and instead came down to Huddersfield to stay with me for a couple of days. He then shocked me by buying a house in Waterloo, phoned Mum up and told her to put the house on the market as they were moving down here. I think he had a sixth sense and wanted Mum to be near me in case something happened to him.

I suspect he also felt a bit depressed in Scotland as all his friends were dying – he was forever at funerals – and deliberately chose an estate in Huddersfield which had young families living there so it was full of life.

I made him chairman as he had a strong sense of structure and discipline and was an exceedingly wise man with great knowledge about people. He was the seventh child of a seventh child which seemed to give him some kind of special insight. Put it this way, when we were growing up he knew if either me or my sister was lying to him simply by looking at us. If I told him I'd been to the youth club he'd say: "No, you haven't, you've been to the café." And he was always right.

He'd served in India during the war and the only time we ever saw him cry was when we drove along the coast in Scotland and he spotted the *Georgic* – the ship that brought him home from India – being scrapped. He stopped the car and sobbed.

Galpharm had been going for a year and we decided to have a celebration at Woodsome Golf Club at Fenay Bridge and on that day I was in a meeting with bank manager Bob Riley when I got a call from my sole employee at work, Arthur Haigh, to say I had to go to my parents' home immediately.

The tone in his voice made me realise it was serious so I immediately left the meeting and drove quickly there. Sadly, it was too late. Dad had already died in my mother's arms from a heart attack.

He was 72 and had been such a calming influence on me. I could be hot-headed and impulsive at times and once wrote a letter to fax to a customer after we'd had a difference of opinion. It was passionate and forthright, but Dad read it, said 'Tear it up and write a proper one in the morning.' I did and the next one was totally different after I'd calmed down. Everyone needs a calming influence at times and mine was my dad.

My mum, Anne, never got over losing him and wrote: "When a marriage is shattered by the death of the husband, especially if it was sudden, the euphemisms may comfort such as 'it was best for him' but the knowledge remains that nothing will be the same for the one who is left and who loved him most. How does one set about living without him after falling in love with a chap on sight and staying in love with him for nearly 45 years?"

And she wrote a note for us to read when she died in January 2006 aged 89 which was headlined 'On My Decease', which said: "Goodbye my family. My life is past. I loved you all to the very last. Weep not for me but courage take. Love each other for my sake, for those who love don't go away, they walk beside you every day."

Another great asset to Galpharm's early days was my first employee, Arthur Haigh. He'd been a mill manager in charge of a large workforce but had been made redundant and was recommended to me by Alf Wellings who owned the mill at Aspley which had become Galpharm's new base.

Arthur had the same birthday as me, August 5, although was older in his mid-50s and I knew within 30 seconds of meeting him he'd be a great employee. And he was.

Arthur took on everything from invoicing to deliveries and was responsible for all products coming in and out of Galpharm. But, above all else, he was probably the most naturally happy person I've ever met, had a song for every occasion and played trombone in a swing band. We held all our management meetings in the Flyboat pub around the corner.

Arthur was also a thinker. We bought a 7-tonne Luton Bedford truck for Arthur to take our products to customers countrywide, especially in the Birmingham and London areas, and then drove the empty truck back. He realised there must be companies around here who needed stock bringing back and his wife worked in the accounts at Huddersfield pharmaceutical company Thornton and Ross. She mentioned it at work and they did often need stuff collecting and bringing back here from the south and the Midlands. So did Superdrug, so Arthur's enterprising idea ended up turning in a handsome profit transporting stock for other companies.

It meant that every time he made a delivery Arthur would ask in his broad Yorkshire accent: "Have you owt that needs tekin' back up north?"

Never stop thinking in business or looking for an opportunity.

Sometimes it may be staring you in the face, yet you don't see it straightaway, which is why every employee should always be encouraged to pitch in with ideas.

I really liked Alf who owned the mill. The time came for a rent review and we were paying very little but he refused to put it up the whole time we were there, saying: "Nay lad, tis fun havin' thee here."

He walked us through his mill one day and I spotted a man asleep beneath a newspaper. Alf said: "I pay him to be asleep. He's the electrician. When he's asleep the machines are working and when he's awake he's working and the machines aren't."

The first product we provided was lip balm. A buyer from Superdrug called Mike Travis was fed up paying the high prices demanded by big established brands and wanted to launch his own Superdrug brand in its stores. Mike asked if I could source it and research took me to three companies – in Spain, Germany and Finland. The ones in Germany and Spain were manufacturing a brand called Labello which would have brought them into direct conflict, but the Finland factory, Oy Bergenheim, was definitely a goer and they made lip balm for skiers so we knew it must be good.

Within a year they'd produced one million lip balms for Superdrug in four flavours – vanilla, strawberry, Coca-Cola and mint. To mark such a brilliant first year I went to JPB Jewellery on Half Moon Street in Huddersfield and commissioned them to make a gold replica of the Superdrug lip balm which I gave to them.

This also gave us the business formula to make new products which would shape Galpharm strategy for the next 30 years and we still use it in business today.

These are the four clear steps.

Secure an inquiry from a buyer and ensure that initial quantities mean we would break even after three months.

Develop our own formula for the product and with our own lip balm we brought in researchers from Aston University in Birmingham who devised a lip balm that protected the lips better than other brands. Their microscopes revealed the lips have tiny crevasses so it was vital the lip balm was soft to get right into them otherwise people would be left suffering from blisters. We also included a sun protection so the lips would be protected if people were either skiing or sitting on a camel in the Sahara.

Select a manufacturer with a proven track record.

Come up with a good name and make the pack design striking.

Our lip balm was called Lipmate – a name suggested by my second wife Ann – and I'd asked female buyers to give me a kiss on the tissue to get the perfect lips image for the packaging.

In the end the lip balm was the first one to give protection from the sun, it was half the price of the main big brand alternative, Lypsil, the first to have different flavours and the first own brand lip balm in the UK.

It meant we were up and running.

Galpharm starts to grow with weird things happening along the way

Opportunity is the watchword of business.

Essential reading for me was the *Chemist and Druggist Directory* – not exactly a page-turner for most folk but it was for me. The reason was it listed all pharmaceuticals and also if they were available by prescription only, sold in pharmacies or were on general sale.

It's amazing how many were on the General Sales List so could be bought anywhere such as supermarkets, corner shops and cash and carry warehouses. Some manufacturers made them pharmacy only which restricted outlets and helped them to keep prices high. No-one else seemed to be spotting this opportunity.

You can get some chancers in business and one turned up at Wallis Laboratory when I was there in my consultancy role.

A bloke arrived with a suitcase full of cash and wanted Wallis to manufacture his 'instant slimming pill' and he'd pay £200,000 for them to do so.

As with all things in life, if it sounds too good to be true then it usually is and his sales pitch was that all people had to do was take two of his magical slimming pills at night before going to bed and by the morning they'd have lost weight.

He sounded more like one of the old-time quack doctors and analysis of his pills showed they contained nothing more than edible chalk. The thing is that people naturally lose weight while sleeping so it could fool quite a few into thinking it worked.

The conman wanted to charge £28 a box but was quickly shown the door. Our business philosophy was to build companies with strong reputations and longevity. His was to con and run.

The next time we saw him was when Esther Rantzen exposed him on BBC consumer watchdog programme *That's Life* which ran from 1973 to 1994.

Another great comic moment came from a man who had invented formulas for some medicines and wanted Wallis to manufacture them.

He proudly showed us his first product, an analgesic for pain he called Phorpain.

I then asked if he had any other formulas we could look at for potential future development.

He sure had – a cough linctus.

"Oh, really. What's that called?" I asked.

Completely straight-faced he said it was called Phorcough, totally unaware what it sounded like when he said it out loud.

Both Paul and I struggled to contain our giggles.

It then became like that great scene in *Monty Python's Life of Brian* when Julius Caesar reveals the name of his friend, Biggus Dickus, and, when asked to say what Biggus's wife is called, all the guards fall about howling with laughter when it's revealed to be Incontinentia Buttocks.

Well, we then asked him if he had anything else in his medicinal pipeline. We weren't to be disappointed as he was working on a cream to reduce swelling on the skin.

We hardly dared ask him what this was called, but couldn't resist. He replied excitedly: "Phorskin."

We had to leave the boardroom with tears rolling down our faces.

Phorpain did actually become a product – not done by Wallis – but as for Phorskin it was a case of Phorcough.

Galpharm did though turn down a golden opportunity which we certainly wouldn't have done with the gift of hindsight.

A friend came to see me in 1986 and asked if I wanted to be the northern distributor for bottled water called Evian sourced in the French Alps.

I was gobsmacked. We live in one of the wettest places in England where free water pours from the tap. Why on earth would anyone want to pay for water from a bottle?

Time has proved me very wrong with that one.

Our distribution by this point was into what the Americans called drug stores and there were four main ones then in England – Superdrug, Tip Top Stores, Medicare, Share Drug and, in Scotland, Semichem.

This was run by Scottish entrepreneur Drew Kerr, a brilliant bloke who tried every new product I offered, except one.

I phoned him to say I had a special offer on Wilkinson Sword's new razor called Retractor.

He said: "Graham, I've got a warehouse full of toilet rolls."

I replied: "Go on, just take a pallet of razors and I'll do you sale or return."

Drew said: "You're not understanding, laddie. I've got a warehouse full of toilet rolls."

I was still trying to work out what he meant when he explained: "If they're not wiping their arses, they're certainly not going to shave."

I couldn't resist a sideline so did some car trading between 1982 and 1985 and ended up driving a mustard-coloured Volvo Sports P1800 S – the same model driven by TV gentleman adventurer Simon Templar.

I felt I was on the right road in every sense of the word. Our customers had come to need us rather than buying from us as we were so much cheaper than buying the brand names directly from the manufacturer.

It's known as a 'reliance relationship' when customers become reliant on you. I think of reliance relationships as the Rolls Royce of selling. Put simply, buy right, sell right and deliver on time.

The brands I was getting from friendly pharmacy wholesalers and then selling on included Bic, Gillette and Wilkinson razors, Sudocrem antiseptic healing cream, Oraldene for minor mouth infections and Redoxon to treat and prevent vitamin C deficiency. Up to now they'd only been sold in pharmacies but we'd found a whole new market by selling them over the counter in grocery stores and other shops.

Sudocrem was particularly massive for us as we managed to get a Discrete Distribution Agreement with the manufacturer in Ireland to sell it far and wide. Up to then it had been available only through pharmacies and Boots was beginning to demand a higher cost price.

So we sold it discretely through the cash and carry network and were soon shifting pallet loads every week.

That loyalty was repaid. When they were about to sell Sudocrem to an American company they allowed me to buy a year's stock as they thought the new owners wouldn't sell it to me but I didn't have to pay for the best part of the year.

The owner flew over to Leeds Bradford Airport, came to see me, thanked me for all my business over the previous five years or so and gave me a document before he left. I later realised it was the formula for Sudocrem – what a wonderful gesture. It's safely locked away and I've never done anything with it.

Business was growing, so much so that by 1985 I had a couple more employees – Patricia who sorted out all the administration and Russell. Now Russell wasn't his real name but I called him that because he was always repacking things and there always seemed to be the sound of rustling going on in the warehouse.

I also started with a new rule for taking on more employees. Sales had to grow by an extra £500,000 to justify each new appointment. It remained that ratio right until I sold Galpharm in 2008.

I'd started with help from a bank loan but I've never been a big fan of banks as they have the power to bust businesses. The traditional model of funding businesses though was still to go to the banks cap in hand.

They'd want assets in return for lending money so people are in constant danger of losing their homes and if the business goes into administration or liquidation the banks would sell the stock for a fraction of its real value ... around 20%.

Galpharm was different as we often had £2m in branded stock. There would never be any reason to drop the price as our customers relied on us and without our stock they'd have empty shelves. There could even be an argument that if Galpharm was going bust the prices would actually increase as that would be the last they'd be able to get from us.

In the severe recession of 1979 a pal of mine shot himself after his business went to the wall. Another lost everything and never worked again. Running a business can be horrendously stressful.

My great accountant, Melvyn Hoyle, advised me to set up my own Self-Administered Pension Scheme (SASS) in 1986 and we began by putting £8,000 in it. A few weeks later he said he'd received £6,000 which was his commission from the pension company for setting up the scheme. The sky-high commissions were seemingly justified because the pension company would benefit over the years from my money.

Melvyn said he was embarrassed by the high commission and wanted me to have it but, in the end, we split it 50/50.

I got 40% tax relief on the pension but could also borrow up to 50% of the scheme back into Galpharm at any time. As Galpharm became more successful I placed half my profits into the scheme. This became the most tax efficient and safest way to finance Galpharm's future and we used it to fund Galpharm's expansion over the next 25 years – kind of like our own bank.

It's also the pension for my retirement which hasn't happened yet and I'm beginning to wonder if it ever will.

The pension fund also helped us to ride out a couple of recessions without relying on banks to help.

As it is, four things still traditionally sell well during recessions – pharmaceuticals (as people will still be in pain), chocolate (little treats really count), alcohol (to relax and forget), baby stuff (you'll often see a baby boom in a recession with people having more time on their hands).

When people talk to me about banks I'll usually tell them that even Jesus threw the money lenders out of the temple ... and he had good reason to do so.

The only time we borrowed from the bank was in 1993 when we bought almost £1m of branded razor blades and said we'd repay within six weeks. All the money was paid back within a month.

The search was now on to expand the product range and expand Galpharm into a major player in the pharmaceutical industry.

Whisky, women and razor blades with a couple of Peaky Blinders moments

Superdrug was formed by Ralph Goldstein who started out as a barrow boy in London.

By the time I met him in 1982 he had a chain of 150 branches with the headquarters in Croydon near Croydon Airport which was Britain's first international airport and the place where Amy Johnson and other flight pioneers took off on their record-breaking exploits.

The first time I met Ralph was certainly one to remember as he tried to nail me down on price in a friendly yet crafty way.

I was down in the Croydon headquarters with one of the Superdrug buyers when Ralph came past, stopped, looked at me and said: "I believe I owe you a cheque. Stop by my office before you leave and I'll write it out for you."

They certainly did owe me money and it was quite a big one but the buyer, Mike Travis, warned me: "If I were you I'd just beggar off home. If you end up in the boss's office then it's going to cost you."

But before I could escape Ralph was back downstairs and led me up to his office where the cheque book was neatly laid out on the table ready to be signed.

Great, I thought. All he has to do is write it out and I'll be off up north.

But it wasn't going to be that simple.

"Would you like a whisky?" asked Ralph.

"No, I'm fine," I replied, knowing I had a long drive ahead of me.

"Oh, go on," said Ralph. "I'm having one and I can't drink on my own."

So I caved in, thinking I could get away with just one drink. That was naïve.

Ralph just chatted generally for around 20 minutes and gave me another drink … and then another.

He was knocking his back but I started to look for an escape route for my whisky other than into my mouth, so tipped it into a nearby plant every time he wasn't looking.

"You certainly seem to like the whisky," said Ralph, noticing that my glass was emptying as quickly as his own.

He eventually got down to business. We'd started to stock the

Galpharm lip balm in Superdrug so Ralph had suddenly become familiar with my company's name.

"I've checked up on you and discovered we account for nearly 45% of your business," he said. "Your cash flow will be shot if I don't write you this cheque."

And then came the rub. He said he'd write the cheque there and then rather than waiting for the usual 30 days … but as I'd be getting it so soon he'd knock off a 10% 'settlement discount'.

I replied that if he did that he'd wipe out all my profit margin.

But he wasn't giving up that easily, adding: "Have another whisky then give me an earner, a little tickle."

By that he meant a price reduction but I stood my ground. Ralph then dropped to 7.5% and finally 5% but I absolutely refused.

In the end he backed down and wrote me the cheque in full.

By then I'd drunk way too much to drive so had to spend some of it staying in a hotel overnight. But it was worth it.

People are what make a business and I was very lucky to have a very steady hand in Galpharm which belonged to my accountant, Melvyn Hoyle. He was loyal, upstanding and unflappable in a crisis until the day someone tried to carry out a hit on him in the centre of Holmfirth.

It all started when I was looking to buy a company in South Yorkshire in the late 1980s that produced a wonder slimming drink that was supposed to replace meals.

It was on the market for £500,000 which seemed a good price so I started to negotiate terms.

But then Melvyn started what he called his 'Yorkshire ferret' due diligence into the company to make sure everything was above board.

What he discovered was that it was well below board. The company chairman had more than 20 other businesses which seemed respectable on the surface but were all registered offshore in the British Virgin Islands and Melvyn found it was a money laundering operation turning drugs money into clean money.

They did this by buying small and medium-sized enterprises on the UK Stock Exchange and then selling them for way less than they were worth. The one I was interested in was valued at £1.5m so they were only asking for a third of the price.

During the time he was looking into the business Melvyn was walking through Holmfirth when he was approached by two men who suggested he backed off with his investigations or they would sort him, his wife and his kids out.

Melvyn told them where to go in no uncertain terms and carried on to his office in Holmfirth but when he left a short time later to go home a car drove down the pavement at him and he had to leap for his life. He went straight to his lawyers, made a will and brought a copy to me to keep safe for him.

I spoke to a lawyer who knew the man selling the company on the cheap.

He said: "Don't have anything to do with him. He's a crook so forget the deal."

The deal was immediately dropped but never forgotten.

By this time we started to realise that razor blades were an incredibly valuable commodity. Millions of people use them but there were only about five main players at the time – Gillette, Wilkinson Sword, Bic, India-based Malhotra and the American Safety Razor Company.

We were distributing Wilkinson replacement packs of double-edged blades on their behalf through cash and carry warehouses and, ultimately, corner shops. It made more sense to Wilkinson for us to do that to save employing reps to do it themselves, especially as we already had all the contacts and we even started to sell them in Africa and the Middle East.

Then Wilkinson brought out a new disposable product called a retractor blade and the managing director said he had an agent in New York who could sell eight containers into the USA.

I said I could sell more than that through a network I'd built up over there so he paid for a flight and a hotel in Manhattan for a week for me and told me to get on with it.

I met up with an Irish trader based near Marbella in Spain called Peter Gallagher who sold Bic razors and was going to a trade fair in New York at the same time. His claim to fame was that he married the first female model to pose topless at the Motor Show.

An Englishman and an Irishman in New York. Time for some fun. After all, it was Super Bowl Day 1989.

We went to the famous Rosie O'Grady's bar and restaurant near Times Square. There was a large group of women in there who were having a few drinks before going to the theatre. I was wearing a see-though skeleton watch and a lady saw it and remarked on how much she liked it.

"That's very kind of you to say so," I said in my best English accent.

"Oh my God, you're English," she replied. We got chatting and the next minute Peter, who was standing at the bar waiting for his whiskey, was deluged by 20 overly excited American women heading in his direction.

"What on earth have you told them?" he gestured and mouthed to me, as we couldn't hear one another over the noise in the bar.

I mouthed back: "I've told them you walk the Queen's corgis."

He quickly cottoned on and didn't let them down, spinning some right yarns such as the route he took the corgis on in Hyde Park and the secret back entrance to Buckingham Palace he used.

Mightily impressed and falling for every word, the women then invited us to events all weekend, including a Super Bowl party. In the end I confessed to one of them that the corgis tale had been made up, trying to explain it was all down to our quirky British sense of humour.

"Don't tell a soul," she said. "They won't find it funny."

In the end, I sold just short of 60 containers of Wilkinson disposable retractor blades into the US.

Around this time Wilkinson had heard of a man called Irwin Armstrong setting up a razor blade factory in Northern Ireland called Smart Razors and asked if I could find out more about his operation.

Turns out he'd developed a single-edged disposable razor very similar to Bic and was looking for a UK-wide distributor. A classic case of right place and right time as we went on to work closely together for many years.

But I also had a marketing gem up my sleeve … the first disposable razor made specially for women. At that time women used to borrow their partner's razors to get rid of unwanted hair from, literally, everywhere. Thing is, hair follicles are different in different areas of the body and a bit of highly personal shaving by the ladies often left the gents' razors blunt.

They knew their wives had been using their razors when it suddenly pulled their own skin back.

There was also the risk of cross infection, especially if the razors went from women's bits to men's cheeks without a thorough clean. You get the picture.

So we came up with the Lady Amanda disposable razor named after my daughter and it was pink to make it clear on the shelves and in the bathroom that it wasn't for men.

The razor took the market by storm and it was the first of its kind, again ahead of the curve.

Irwin was looking at setting up a razor-making factory in Bulgaria to cut his costs and wanted me to go with him as a consultant. It was a once-only business trip there and what happened made me vow to never go again.

During the trip we ended up being wined and dined by the Russian mafia where everyone – even the kitchen staff – had guns.

The next day the head of the mafia turned up in the reception at our hotel, the Hilton in Sofia, with two armed bodyguards looking like Hugo Boss models and a couple of glamorous molls.

He had a proposal for me as he'd heard I was known as The Pharmacist. He said he'd sell me a pharmaceutical factory in Bulgaria for $3m – reasonably inexpensive for a factory – but it turned out there was a catch. We'd have to pay him $2m in protection money every year.

Or, as he put it with a wry smile: "To make sure everything continues to work well."

I refused his kind offer but thanked him all the same for thinking of me.

I was pretty relieved to get out of the country.

The only time I was in real danger was in a taxi on the Crumlin Road in Northern Ireland on my way to see Irwin at the height of The Troubles.

A rocket flashed across the road in front of us and slammed into a nearby Ford dealership, blowing it up.

Although not aimed at me I was advised to grow my hair so there was no chance of me being mistaken for a British squaddie as I was there so often.

Point taken and I grew it so long I ended up with a ponytail.

The day I flew with the world's dodgiest pilot

In the late 1980s I was scheduled to go to a business meeting in Wexford, southern Ireland, one autumn.

It was a company I had invested in and was a UK advisor on the board.

It wasn't the easiest place to get to at that time as usually I'd need to fly into Dublin from Manchester or Leeds Bradford airport and then hire a car to drive the 100 miles or so down to Wexford.

But someone in a travel agents reckoned they could sort me out with a direct flight from Huddersfield International Airport to Waterford Airport near Wexford.

When we say international airport that may be over-egging it a tad. Huddersfield only has a small private airfield on a moor called Crosland Hill but I suppose it was international as people could fly overseas in their own aircraft.

Turned out I'd been booked to fly with a pilot in his small two-seater Cessna-style aircraft from Crosland Hill direct to Waterford Airport.

He looked more like a country and western singer than a pilot, was in his mid-40s with ginger hair and wore a checked shirt. The medication in his top left shirt pocket rattled as we rumbled along ready for take-off, which was slightly unnerving.

We set off down the runway and I knew that if the pilot got it wrong at Crosland Hill the plane would end up nose first in a quarry. He managed to get off the ground ... but only just.

He turned to me and said with a wry grin: "That was a bit tight – it must be the weight from the extra load."

I'd no idea what extra load he was talking about but then I heard a noise behind us and his girlfriend appeared from among the luggage. She'd been hiding there as she wasn't on the manifest.

"Weird," I thought.

It then got weirder as the pilot got out an AA road map of the UK and tried to prop it on the dashboard before it tumbled to the floor.

"Right, let's look for the M1," he said, picking it up and trying to rest it on his knee.

Needless to say, worry was starting to set in by this point as he followed the motorway and then turned right to go across Birmingham and Wales.

He then said: "Do you want to have a go at flying?" and insisted I take over the controls.

I'd never flown a plane before so just took a firm grip and tried to keep it in a straight line as the pilot had a coffee break and also took some of his tablets.

"Don't worry, it's just normal medication," he said as he took over flying again.

I began to worry what he classed as normal medication.

By this time we were leaving the English coast behind and heading out over the Irish Sea.

"How long before we reach Ireland?" I asked.

"Oh, about 20 minutes," he replied.

After about 25 minutes had passed all we could still see was more sea.

"I think we've missed Ireland," I said. "I reckon we've gone too far south. You need to head north."

At first he wasn't so sure and was inclined to carry on but he did turn north and the manoeuvre proved me right. Eventually we found Ireland and, probably more by luck than judgement, he managed to get us over Waterford which is close to Wexford.

He asked for permission to land at the small aerodrome at Waterford but they asked who he was and his flight number. The control tower clearly wasn't expecting him.

He carried on regardless and when he spotted a gap in the cloud dived down and landed. He parked the plane, clambered out and was promptly arrested. The police took his girlfriend away too but let me go when I proved I was a legitimate businessman off to a meeting about water purifying tablets at a company called Medentech Ltd in Wexford.

I returned to the airport the next morning for the flight home and a pilot who was about to take off in his own plane came up to me and asked if I was with the bloke who had been arrested the previous day.

When I said I was, he replied: "I wouldn't go back with him if I was you, especially as there's a cold front looming with bad weather and you don't want to be flying a small aircraft through that. Hire a car to Dublin and get a proper flight home."

I took his advice.

Last I heard was the dodgy pilot I flew down with later took off to fly back to England with his girlfriend but the plane vanished and they were never seen again.

How buying some razors ended up with a police raid

By now Galpharm was growing quickly, boosted by its ever-increasing product range and the fact it was selling its own tubs of 25 paracetamol for 35p while people were still being charged £1.29 for the same amount of Panadol in Boots.

We'd started off as opportunist traders but had grown a range of products and customers had come to rely on us to provide them at the right price. In effect, we'd started cost-effective healthcare and our slogan was 'We Cover Both Ends' from headache tablets to anti-diarrhoea medication.

We needed bigger premises so turned to my pension scheme – our so-called Bank of Galpharm – for help, which paid £180,000 for offices and 7,000 square ft of warehouse space on Foundry Street just off Birds Royd Lane in Brighouse. We left Firth Street in Huddersfield in 1985 and there were four of us in the company when we moved in.

We paid rent back to the pension scheme at the rate of £18,000 a year but eventually sold the premises for £250,000 when we made a far bigger move later, so it was a nice little earner for the pension fund in the end.

I'd proved the concept correct. We could expand without worrying about risk ... or banks. It was the pension scheme making the investments, run totally separately from the company. It was only my pension that was at stake.

One of the biggest razor blade companies in the world was Malhotra based in India who bought their raw steel from Sheffield and they wanted to interview me about possibly selling their twin disposable razor under the brand name Laser – a direct rival to the Gillette blue twin – to help them expand into the UK market.

It was to be no ordinary interview as the company was run by Dr Naveen Malhotra, but I had to meet and be approved by his father and grandfather who by then was in his 80s.

Their home took up around half of Grosvenor Square just off Park Lane in London and it was like a palace inside. I was led into the throne room where the grandfather, who had created the Malhotra business empire, was sitting on a raised gold chair.

To give an indication as to how wealthy and important this

family had become, there was a photo of the grandfather with Joseph Kennedy – John F Kennedy's father and American ambassador to the British Isles – signing a lease to rent the premises for the American Embassy in Grosvenor Square from the Malhotra family in 1946, the year I was born.

I knew I needed to connect with them so chatted about my father's military service in India during World War Two and his love of the food out that there meant I was brought up on Indian curries in Middlesbrough in the 1950s – long before Indian restaurants opened in the town.

I was fascinated by Indian history too, especially how Ghandi had led the country to break free from British rule and the way the country had moved on since then.

The grandfather asked how I got into razor blades and after a few minutes he simply got up and walked out. That was the sign that I'd passed the interview and the family would do business with Galpharm.

They were very powerful and well-connected people and also extremely loyal when it came to business.

They were also very much a family-orientated company and that's what Galpharm became. My son, Craig, went straight to work after leaving Holmfirth High after getting a job as a trainee salesman for Wilkinson Sword.

His role was initially a trainee salesman, was successful very quickly, was promoted to salesman with his own territory and by his mid-20s was the company's youngest ever regional manager and then national sales manager before leaving for a brief spell at Jeyes in another senior management role.

A colleague had left Wilkinson and was doing well at Vileda Mops and was trying to poach Craig over to Vileda.

Craig came to see me for some advice and I told him Galpharm was taking off and I was struggling to do all the selling myself. We discussed him joining the family firm but I still wasn't convinced the company would survive in the long-term in such a competitive market so wondered if it would ultimately be a wise move for him.

Yet Craig said: "I'll always sell. I'll never starve."

So he joined Galpharm in April 1991 on half the salary he'd been on before but with a great performance-related incentive package so he could potentially earn far more.

It also eventually led to several of Craig's former Wilkinson Sword workmates moving across to Galpharm. It's always best to employ people if you already know how good they are, their strengths and that they've a proven track record in sales. We called it TT – tried and tested.

In business things can sometimes go wrong, never more so than when the police raided the Galpharm business and our homes.

It was all to do with a consignment of Gillette razor blades.

Craig did all the buying for Galpharm but had gone away on honeymoon in Bermuda. While he was away I bought £80,000 worth of Gillette blades from one of our usual suppliers and sold them to Morrisons supermarket. It was just a typical deal at the time.

About a month later I was in the dentist's chair having treatment around 2.30pm when an urgent call came through saying I needed to get back to the office straightaway. I told Craig I wouldn't be long but he said I had to return immediately and there was panic in his voice. No matter what pain I was enduring in the dentist's, seemingly it was nothing to what was going on there.

I arrived in Brighouse 15 minutes later to find a police van and around four police cars at the office. Craig was ashen-faced and my lawyer, Paul Booth from my Huddersfield solicitors Baxter Caulfield, had arrived looking very serious.

The police said Craig and I were both under arrest and the office along with my home, Knole House on Northgate in Honley, were being searched as part of an investigation into allegedly counterfeit Gillette blades that we'd sold to Morrisons.

Turns out Gillette had taken out what's known as an Anton Piller injunction against Galpharm, a court order that gives the right to search premises and seize evidence with no warning. This is to stop any evidence being hidden or destroyed and is often used in cases of alleged trademark, copyright or patent offences.

Gillette had tracked the blades from eastern Europe through the supply chain and right to Morrisons where they had bought a pack and their tests revealed they were counterfeit. This meant I was under suspicion of being the Mr Big in an international counterfeit razor blade scam, especially as I'd represented Smart Razors, Laser Razors, Wilkinson Sword trading razors and had looked at buying a factory in Bulgaria.

Paul Booth was calm, quiet and reassuring and argued we should have been told about the legal proceedings before so we could have explained what had happened.

As it was we'd bought them in good faith from what we thought was a trusted supplier and had no idea they were anything but genuine Gillette blades.

So I wasn't the Mr Big they thought I was and we were eventually allowed to trade in Gillette razor blades again.

But Craig barred me from buying again. Ever.

His strengths were buying, supply and logistics. Mine were ideas, innovation, sales and marketing.

And that's a valuable lesson in business. Stick to what you know.

How the danger of 'passing off' was cheekily ahead of the curve

I had two great ideas to mirror a couple of household names and both ended, well, disappointingly.

The first involved the massive brand Fisherman's Friend throat lozenges.

We came up with a very similar product at Galpharm, but what to call it? I came up with Bosun's Mate, thinking it was really rather clever but was met by a stony silence in the boardroom.

Still, as boss I had the final decision but thought I'd ask the Fisherman's Friend owner, Doreen Lofthouse, if she'd mind. Turned out Doreen minded very much, for the next thing to arrive in the office was a letter from her solicitor threatening legal action. Their company was so big they'd have the money and power to take out an injunction, freeze our accounts and even seize assets, which isn't exactly good for business or our reputation. At that time we were a minnow to their shark and my assets were not much more than a guitar, a sailing boat and a budgie.

Doreen was an incredibly charity-minded person and when she died in March 2021 aged 91 she left her £41m fortune to improve her home town of Fleetwood and had previously given millions of pounds to community projects in Lancashire.

Talking of things nautical, my other 'great' idea was to launch a brand of cod liver oil and multivitamins to rival well-known brand Seven Seas, but we'd call ours Five Oceans.

Let's just say the idea struggled to swim before sinking without trace.

Passing off is everywhere nowadays, especially the budget supermarkets with Aldi launching its Aldidas range playing on the Adidas brand in 2022, yet back then we didn't have the money or company size to be able to stand our ground.

We had a different name, a different formula and a different supplier.

It was a case of I didn't have the money nor the balls at the time.

The memorable day Galpharm really took off

In the late 1980s Galpharm was taken to another level with the creation of our own research and development company called Healthy Ideas Ltd ... and part of it happened by chance.

I was in the White Hart pub at New Mill near Holmfirth, right in the heart of *Last of the Summer Wine* country, and got chatting to a bloke at the bar. His name was Ian Kirk who was a very talented research chemist looking for a new challenge. He was the right man in the right place – the pub – at the right time.

He ended up joining us in the venture along with Peter Cox, ex-managing director of pharmaceutical manufacturers Wallis Laboratory and he brought in Andy Hunkin who was an expert on regulations and how to make submissions for product licences to Medicines Control Agency which has now become the Medicines and Healthcare Products Regulatory Agency.

Our aim was to look at ways to switch medicines from prescription only and those sold exclusively in pharmacies to general sale in supermarkets and shops, making them far easier for people to buy and way less expensive.

The culture at Healthy Ideas was just that – exceptionally healthy – as we all had clearly defined roles and were committed to working together to drive Galpharm forward with Craig and I managing the sales, marketing, supply and distribution, while Peter took care of the manufacturing.

We were kind of like the five medical buccaneers and time showed we were definitely ahead of the curve!

We were a close-knit team with clear goals in mind ... to be the first to market with over-the-counter medicine sales and would do this by always asking that all-important question, why.

Why were so many medicines only available by prescription or through pharmacies? Did they need to be and what needed to be done to challenge, disrupt and change that market which would make medicines so easy to buy.

In short, our quest was to make affordable medicines through Galpharm with the company ultimately the UK's largest supplier. That's what we set out to do and, in the end, thankfully, that's what we achieved.

We were a streamlined organisation – a speedboat compared to the huge pharmaceutical companies who I regarded as tankers. By this I meant they were large, cumbersome organisations shackled by policies and procedures that were very slow to change direction, while we could make quick decisions and U-turn immediately if something wasn't working for us or we suddenly wanted to pursue a new opportunity. That speed was all important in maintaining and enhancing our market position.

One of the first innovative things we did was to turn some medicines into double action such as combining cough medicine with a decongestant or a cough medicine with an antihistamine to help people to get a good night's sleep.

We were the forerunners in dual relief medicines which are now commonplace. Back then they simply didn't exist.

We were also groundbreaking as we turned to scientists at the University of Bradford to help us with development and research. We'd not heard of a university being involved before so this was revolutionary in the early 1990s.

We were also ahead of the curve by discovering what the big brands were developing next and then having our own genetic brand ready to go as soon as they released theirs.

How we found out so far in advance what our competitors were doing was down to trademark registration. They'd register an extension to a current product – perhaps a new cough remedy flavour – to protect their trademark and by doing so unknowingly allowing us access to their future marketing plans. We'd then go away and develop our own at speedboat pace.

We also paid for our research scientists to go to conferences where they met research scientists from the big brands and some couldn't help bragging about what they were going to launch next after a few drinks at the bar.

One we did was our own hot lemon drink which came out, coincidentally, at the same time one of the biggest pharmaceutical suppliers in the world, Reckitt and Colman, launched theirs. Although you may not be familiar with the company, its history stretches back to 1840 and you'll know their brands such as Nurofen, Gaviscon, Strepsils, Clearasil and, er, Durex.

In the late 1980s they'd brought out a hot lemon drink and we were aware they were researching and manufacturing it so we produced one of our own at speedboat pace.

We sorted out our own artwork and produced our own hot lemon drink for Lloyds pharmacies – the second largest pharmacy chain in the UK after Boots. It was nice, eye-catching packaging in green with a lemon on. Everyone seemed happy with it – except Reckitt and Colman who reckoned it was too similar to their design. They complained it was a copy and accused us of passing off, which meant the packaging was so similar customers were picking ours up by mistake even though it was also around a third cheaper.

In short, they said it was causing confusion on the shelves and could potentially sue Galpharm for loss of profits.

That's when the Lloyds buying director at the time stepped in and solved the problem. Galpharm brands were selling well in all the Lloyds stores and they were keen to develop their own brand range with us so he didn't want the boat rocking. He did something unusual yet powerful by delisting several Reckitt and Colman brands, including the hot lemon. This meant they were cleared from the shelves so there would no longer be any risk of confusion.

The problem was solved for us but it left Reckitt and Colman facing a far bigger one. They needed to be back on the Lloyds shelves and fast so applied to Lloyds to be listed again. Lloyds agreed but it came with a price to relist everything again. In the end we think it cost Reckitt and Colman tens of thousands of pounds.

Once our hot lemon became known by Lloyds customers we were able to sell it through other retailers from independent pharmacies to corner shops under the Galpharm brand.

This is the way it worked with all our new products.

Often we'd wait perhaps six months to put our generic products out so customers had seen the new brands, perhaps even tried them but then realised ours were much cheaper yet gave the same relief as they were the same formula or even better than the brand's.

We did this with our paracetamol, ibuprofen, sweeteners, lip balm, razors, cough medicines and antihistamines such as hay fever relief.

Healthy Ideas was so successful it was bought by Galpharm in the mid-1990s with Ian, Andy and Peter becoming Galpharm shareholders and Peter being appointed joint managing director with Craig.

We were lifted into the Premier League of pharmaceuticals one Friday afternoon in June 1995 – the day we proved to the Medicines Control Agency that our generic ibuprofen could be sold in supermarkets and shops rather than only in pharmacies. Up to then ibuprofen was a big pink tablet on prescription and sold by Nurofen but we turned it into a sugar-coated white tablet.

The MCA had to be sure the medicine would benefit the patient and pass efficacy and safety standards – basically that it worked and was completely safe. Data was collected from around the world as well as the UK.

It was the culmination of two years of research, development and thinking differently. For instance, a powerful dose of Nurofen at 400mg could only go through on prescription via the GPs. The Nurofen 200mg were on sale only in pharmacies but at a high cost. But if the Galpharm tablets were only 200mg they could go over the counter so we used that to switch to a general sales list making it available everywhere.

By reducing the ibuprofen pack size to 16 we were allowed to sell it anywhere – the first company in Europe to move a molecule from the legal status of only being sold in pharmacies to be sold in grocers which included the big supermarkets.

We received a fax at our Brighouse headquarters that Friday afternoon and partied hard all weekend as nobody but ourselves fully grasped exactly what we'd achieved and what this moment meant for Galpharm. It was our Holy Grail and from then on we were known as the buccaneers of the pharma industry by launching affordable medicines for everyone.

The next few weeks needed shrouding in secrecy so we would shock the pharmaceutical world when we were ready to launch. We closed our chosen supplier, Sussex Pharmaceuticals, for six weeks while the packaging was printed to say Galpharm's ibuprofen had general sales list status.

We knew no competitor would be able to catch us up for at least a couple of years.

From that day on we became instant major players. Our ibuprofen sold for 49p compared to the big-name brands in the chemists which were £2.19, reaping them vast profits.

The retailers couldn't believe it – at first they thought selling ibuprofen in shops was illegal – but we could assure them it was now perfectly legal and would provide them with their own brands. It opened a whole new sector for them and, instead of us trying to sell to them, they were suddenly coming to us.

Up to this point analgesics such as ibuprofen had only been available in pharmacies and the big manufacturers had become complacent with their market domination.

We'd suddenly opened up a whole new retail world for retailers ... and they loved it. After all, there was no incentive at all for the big brands to do own brands for supermarkets as they'd be cutting their own profit margins.

We also quickly realised how much we were saving the NHS which we reckoned to be around £400m a year through savings on prescriptions of ibuprofen alone with people being able to buy it in supermarkets and other general grocery outlets rather than just at pharmacies.

The way was clear for Galpharm to forge ahead with that full speedboat mentality that served us so well.

We didn't just provide the supermarkets with their own brand medicines, we also offered to sort out their marketing and packaging designs as part of the deal which was often incentive enough for them to sign contracts with us for three years. This meant the factories we used would know they'd have continual orders and secure futures.

Demand grew at such a phenomenal rate we needed more manufacturers on board and so looked beyond the UK.

We learned there were companies in India manufacturing for some of the UK brands so searched there ... and found exactly what we were looking for.

Although, incredibly, there were more than 30,000 generic pharmaceutical manufacturers in India, only around 30 were equipped to meet the UK standards and we put our own Galpharm staff into those we chose to ensure they were meeting both the UK and European compliance and standards. Inspectors from the Medicines Control Agency also went over there to check them out.

Manufacturing costs were so much more economical that by the time I sold Galpharm almost all our medicines were being made in India and we never had a formal supply contract with the factories detailing terms and conditions for buying and delivering the products.

I've always thought that if someone gets a supply contract out of a drawer then it's the beginning of the end of that business relationship as the trust has slipped.

If they ever mentioned concerns over whether they'd be paid then I'd tell them that if we didn't pay them then don't ship the goods, it's as simple as that. Also, I'd get fined by the retailers for leaving them with empty shelves – they relied totally on us to provide their own brand products – so there was every incentive for all of us to stick to our agreement.

Our word was our bond. A handshake and a look in the eye sealed the deals.

Our stock was pre-sold so the factories knew their future orders were assured. One owner said that 80% of his work was now with Galpharm but we needed even more products from him so I helped him to buy another factory so he could increase his production.

Our investment into India and the quality of the products they produced was the bedrock of Galpharm becoming number one, envied by all our competitors.

Most companies with medicinal licences in the UK manufactured products at their own factories.

We didn't have a single factory of our own yet were taking the market by storm and by the time Galpharm was sold in 2008 we had 27 pharmaceutical licences manufacturing at seven different factories.

Our product range was impressive including painkillers, children's medicines, cough and cold remedies, treatments for upset stomachs as well as foot, skin and eye care.

On average, every person in the UK was buying two to three packs of Galpharm medicines every year and eventually we were producing, packaging and distributing more than 75 million paracetamol tablets a month and had a 70% share of the UK's affordable medicines market.

We'd changed everything ... forever.

Why I rejected $11m for Galpharm, but was it the right decision?

The company then went from strength to strength, boosted by some great ideas along the way.

One was Craig's who realised the strength of the medicines could be increased while still keeping them available for sale over the counter, rather than just in pharmacies.

He doubled the strength of our hot lemon paracetamol and called it Max Strength. Genius. No-one else had thought of it at the time.

We were maximising sales of around 60 million paracetamol-based pharmaceuticals and 40 million ibuprofen-based drugs a month with another 75 product variants on sale. Around six in every 10 hay fever and painkillers – including paracetamol and ibuprofen – sold over the counter in the UK were from Galpharm.

One golden rule in business is to never stand still or you'll stagnate, so we were constantly researching and developing potential new products to keep on disrupting the pharmaceutical industry.

I have a saying that money and innovation never sleep.

The man who headed this for us was Richard Eggleston who was head of research and development for another pharmaceutical company, Johnson and Johnson, and when he came to us in search of a new product – a paracetamol elixir for babies – I was very impressed by him. During the second meeting he realised I was kind of interviewing him and during the third meeting I offered him a great salary to join us.

Once he'd agreed I asked him if he'd like to double that salary every year.

"What do I have to do?" he said.

"Provide me with three new products a year," I replied.

It also meant other companies looked enviously at us and one, American company Perrigo, wanted to buy us out even though we weren't for sale. They'd bought a manufacturing plant in the UK and hoped to challenge our market share but it hadn't worked out that way and we'd continued to grow.

One of the directors of Perrigo UK Acquisition Ltd at the time was a rather brash character.

I'd met him once previously when I took him to dinner at the

Dorchester in London and when I said it was my treat he ordered a bottle of wine costing £14,500.

I sent it back and the evening was a rather short one.

In August 2001 he came to the Galpharm head office to meet me and Craig. Once in the boardroom he got his cheque book out, looked at Craig and drawled: "So what will it take so you can disappear into the sunset, sonny."

Craig got up, told the director he couldn't afford us and walked out of the room.

It had sounded more like a threat than an offer and he came up with a figure of $11m even though he'd originally been talking of a higher one.

I called a halt to the meeting and made it clear Galpharm wasn't for sale.

By 2007 I felt my natural drive and passion was starting to ebb away and so I looked to sell. I called in Matt Gooch, head of banking at investment bankers William Blair and Company, to represent us in the sale and he advised us to sell it differently ... by auction so no-one would know what anyone else was offering.

The company had great strengths – market dominance, a strong research and development programme and outsourcing all our manufacturing to tried and trusted companies. We also had a 70% market share in store-branded medicines.

We sent out teaser information – basically all the information about Galpharm already in the public domain such as recent accounts, how much we manufactured for the Galpharm brand and how much for own brand labels, our supply chains, how many new products were in the pipeline and how well we sold against branded products produced by other manufacturers.

We began with several companies showing an interest, quickly narrowed this down to 13 and they were allowed more confidential information before we cut it down to seven serious players.

We whittled that down to three and one was Perrigo. This time it was going to be on our terms, not theirs. We had the market share they wanted and needed. When you're selling something as important as a company, don't be in a position to have to sell as that's when you're more likely to give things away.

Matt told Perrigo that if they wanted Galpharm they'd need to increase their offer by 10% which they did and the other company couldn't match it.

The final figure was $86m – eight times more than we were offered just six years before.

Our Dodworth headquarters – named Hugh House after my dad and built in 1995 – was owned by Galpharm International Ltd Executive Pension Scheme – in short, my own private pension scheme – so they kindly paid rent for the next seven years until they found their own larger premises just around the corner. It still has handprints of my children, Alex and Fay, inset in the concrete on the steps into the building, which they had wanted to do while the concrete was setting when the building was being constructed.

It was a fantastic deal for us as our pre-tax profits at the time were around £3m a year and, although we didn't know it then, the financial crash was just eight months away in September 2008, although traditionally that could lead to a surge in profits for pharmaceutical companies as people use more medicines when they're feeling stressed and low.

The entire auction process began in June 2007 and the sale went through in January 2008 – phenomenally quickly for selling a company of this size.

I now had a product I knew nothing about … a very large amount of cash.

I may have been financially rich beyond my wildest dreams, but danger was lurking just around the corner.

How I almost lost my new-found fortune

By February 2008 I'd sold Galpharm and come into a phenomenal amount of money, but the big question was what to do next.

Craig and I hadn't wanted anyone to know what we'd sold the company for, but Perrigo announced it on the stock market in America that they had made a major investment into the European market and bought Galpharm for $86m. The cat was out of the bag ... and it was a big cat.

Suddenly I was Mr Very Popular, inundated with begging letters and mail from banks, financial companies, charities and, sometimes, just the public telling me what to do with the money and advice on how to invest it. Mostly their ideas seemed to be to invest it with them.

I don't value money and I'm sure people will think that's a strange thing to say. My mum used to declare that a lot of people know the cost of everything but the value of nothing, which I take to mean that people can become all too consumed by materialism and pay silly prices for something that's clearly not worth it.

I'll tell you what I value more and that's friendship, loyalty, integrity, honesty and love. They are the things you should care about in life. I obviously realise that people are struggling so much to make ends meet and to put food on the table and heat in the house and that's why these values are so important to try to get through the tough times and make the most of the happier ones.

I believe that real entrepreneurs don't really give a damn about money. They are born innovators who want to achieve and yearn to be more successful this week than they were the week before, especially for the benefit of the people they had brought in to share the journey with them. They have a passion to succeed and many are philanthropic, giving their time and experience to supporting and encouraging other businesses, charities and organisations.

As Einstein said, only a life lived for others is a life worthwhile.

My knowledge of money was so basic that my accountant at Galpharm, Melvyn Hoyle, drew me three buckets on a piece of paper the first year we made a decent profit. He told me the first was for me, the second was for the company and the third was for the taxman (as they said back then but clearly needs to be taxperson today).

I switched them round putting the company and the need to reinvest in it first, me second but the taxperson still came third. You pay the tax you owe, certainly, but every company does its best to keep that to a minimum. After all, if you don't reinvest in the company the danger is the business will eventually fail and then the taxperson would end up with nothing anyway.

Melvyn simply advised me to concentrate on filling the buckets and he'd sort out the rest. As it was, Galpharm grew every one of its 26 years except for one.

But now it was sold and I was out of there, I had time to think and what I describe as 'hover over my life' for six months. Once you step back from something that was so intensive as running a big business day in and day out it takes time to see it from a distance and make a rational decision about what to do next.

I was 62 but had no intention of retiring.

I did what is known in business as the SWOT analysis and that was to consider the strengths, weaknesses, opportunities and threats in my life. I'd done it for Galpharm every six months and swear by it as the best way to ensure your business remains on track and isn't veering off course. If you go off by one degree and don't recognise what's happening, before you know it you're miles off course and it can be very difficult to get back on track.

We once plotted sailing from New York harbour to Plymouth at just one degree off course … and the boat would have ended up in northern France. Business is the same as sailing – you have to keep on tacking (making corrections) due to the wind, tide and currents as you go to stay right on course for your final destination.

I also needed to be thinking like this when deciding what to do with my money. I've always had a distrust of banks and I'm in the camp that thinks they're often quick to give you an umbrella when it's sunny but just as quick to snatch it away when it starts to rain.

I gave a talk in Leeds to more than 200 very successful Yorkshire business people and enterprising entrepreneurs when a banker who was also speaking tried to convince the audience that bankers were not to blame for the economic crash which shocked the world and ruined lives in 2008.

I was the next speaker up and was supposed to be talking about small and medium business enterprises, but couldn't resist telling them that even Jesus had thrown the money lenders out of the temple and we'd still not learned that lesson today. I sat down but the microphone was still attached to me and the audience overheard the banker turn to me and say: "You t**t." I got a nice round of applause though. In fact, it was quite an ovation.

So what to do with the money.

If you have a large amount then, potentially, it's not 100% safe. In 2007/08 the Financial Services Compensation Scheme only covered the first £35,000 you had with any bank or institution and that moved to £50,000 in 2008 and then became £85,000 in 2010. That's the highest figure you'd be guaranteed of getting back if the bank crashes.

I was with Lloyds but they were keen to tell me that with large amounts to invest they had a private banking section called Mayfair Banking Service offering "enhanced products that offer enhanced rates and rewarding benefits."

I thought this also meant a more secure level of banking and made it clear that this was not 'risk money' – I wanted a safe haven for the money I'd spent my life earning. There was a meeting involving several people at the bank when potential investments were mentioned, especially with American global insurance company American International Group – AIG for short. My money was now with Mayfair Banking but I made it clear at the meeting that no investments should be made without my say so and that meant at least a phone call.

By sheer good fortune there was a senior banking official there and this turned out to be a godsend for me.

At this point in the summer of 2008 I was unaware of the looming disastrous debt crisis in the USA which was threatening the stability of European banks. We first felt this when there was a run on Northern Rock and the British Government had to nationalise the bank to save it.

Interest rates were very low in the USA in the aftermath of the 2001 terror attacks to stimulate the economy and some lenders gave mortgages to people who would not normally get traditional loans because they may have a poor credit history. These were called subprime loans. They were then packaged up and sold on to other financial institutions worldwide as Mortgage Backed Securities – basically high-risk, high-return investments that ultimately crashed spectacularly.

These subprime loans also had a flexible interest rate so when the first signs of a recession started, interest rates went up, the mortgages became more expensive and, on top of that, people began to lose their jobs and couldn't hope to make the payments.

It meant some of the banks and the institutions they'd sold these subprime loans to faced economic meltdown. Even if the banks repossessed the homes, they'd fallen so much in price compared to the loans they'd given to the borrowers they faced enormous losses.

Things took a drastic turn for the worse for the financial world when global financial investment banking firm Lehman Brothers filed for bankruptcy in the USA on the morning of September 15, 2008. This was the fourth largest investment bank in the States with 25,000 employees worldwide and was the climax of the subprime mortgage crisis.

I was in Spain at the time and got a call from one of the bankers at the big meeting I'd had at Mayfair Banking talking about potential investments. He told me it was vital to fax him instructions to remove all my money from AIG that day.

The sense of panic in his voice flowed through my body and I was hit with this sickening feeling that it had all gone. Everything I'd worked so hard for over quarter of a century was lost.

Then I thought, 'What investment with AIG?' I realised I'd never received a call asking me to OK the investment. Although I'd given them three signed blank forms to make investments, the proviso was that all-important phone call first.

It seems that when Lehman Brothers went bust that morning it was in grave danger of taking AIG with it.

Mayfair argued that by providing the blank forms I'd agreed to the investments but that simply wasn't the case and I faced a real battle on my hands. I had a stroke of luck in that on the evening of September 15 the chief executive of the UK arm of AIG had decided to separate his operation from the US parent company which meant it retained some value in it. The result was that around 70% to 80% of my investment should then be repaid after about three years.

The senior banking official who had been at the meeting also helped as he knew about my insistence on a phone call before any investments and that, when it came to money, I was certainly no risk-taking gambler.

He managed to retrieve everything for me eventually but it was an incredibly worrying, stressful and, well, downright scary time. The sense of relief at the end of it all was overwhelming.

If I'd lost everything apart from £50,000 I would have started over again. I don't trust anyone with my finances and, in the years to come, I did actually start again in a sense by investing time, experience and money in other companies and supported several charities because, as I've already stressed, entrepreneurs don't do it for the money, just the passion to succeed.

As I said, banks aren't the safe places you might think they are and, as the 2008 economic crash proved, they're certainly not 'safe as houses'.

The banks caught a severe cold in 2008 and the world ended up with flu.

The day I joined the Huddersfield Town board ... and instantly knew things had to change

I'd always loved playing football right from school.

I was spotted by a Middlesbrough scout and ended up in the Boro reserves in the late 1950s and early 1960s as a right half – that's right midfield to the modern football minds.

My dad was so proud and his imagination was already running riot as he had visions of me playing for England some day.

It was not to be – either for England, Middlesbrough or me.

Even though I knew Linda Shepherdson, daughter of Harold Shepherdson, a Middlesbrough player and manager who went on to be Alf Ramsey's right-hand man when England won the World Cup in 1966, it wasn't enough to save me from being ditched by the club.

I went on trials to Hartlepool when I was about 19 when Brian Clough was manager. He remembered me playing for Middlesbrough and asked me to sign on but by then I'd started as an apprentice hairdresser and my dad said 'no', insisting I finish my apprenticeship instead. Don't forget there was no money in football in those days.

I didn't kick a ball again until I started to play amateur football in Huddersfield in 1971 and joined Berry Brow. I recall being asked to 'laike' for the team and I'd no idea what they were on about, so foolishly said: "I'd rather play football."

I was selected for the team and asked to arrive two hours before kick-off. I thought what dedication – this is a real professional attitude leaving time for training and a warm-up programme before kick-off.

Turns out we were needed early to shift some cows and their cowpats off the pitch before the referee arrived to inspect the field of play. It was more a field of beasts than a field of dreams.

Having kicked off we were quickly awarded a corner which I took as no-one else seemed interested and I soon discovered why. The ball, once placed next to the corner flag, was actually level with the opposition's crossbar because of the heavy slope on the pitch. From then on, playing any team on Leeds Road's gloriously flat playing fields was like playing at Wembley.

I later played for Holmbridge before settling with Wooldale

Wanderers where I later became chairman.

But I'd gone to matches on and off at Town from the early 1970s and by 1989 Town were in the old third division and, after a promising first half of the season under manager Eoin Hand, they'd had a grim second half and lost 2–0 at home to Reading on March 20 which was part of an unenviable run of five defeats at home.

Like all Town fans I was grumbling and was in the Greenall Suite at the ground going on about the board – probably suggesting they didn't know what they were doing – when one of its members, Geoff Headey, overheard me, stopped and said: "Well, if you think you could do a better job why don't you come and join us?"

Days later the chairman, Keith Longbottom, came to see me at the Galpharm office in Brighouse and asked if I wanted to join the board and oversee the commercial operations.

I jumped at the chance.

Just a couple of weeks later football changed forever … and I was there.

It was the ill-fated FA Cup semi-final between Liverpool and Nottingham Forest at Hillsborough and I was in the crowd. One of the Wooldale players was turning 21 and we'd managed to get tickets to celebrate it.

We were sitting in one of the main stands with the Liverpool fans in the stand to our right. They looked packed in, but then again fans were often crammed against one another standing up in those days. When I was a boy watching Middlesbrough in the home end at Ayresome Park – known as the Bob End as it cost a shilling to get in – fans used to pass us down over their heads so we could sit on the wall at the front to watch.

But by 1989 fans were often caged in behind large steel fences known as pens and this was the case at Hillsborough so they couldn't escape the crush when the disaster started.

The game kicked off and, initially, no-one really knew what was happening but then we started to see Liverpool fans clambering onto the pitch. By the time dozens more had spilled onto the grass and we could see people being resuscitated we knew the game was over, a disaster was developing and we left. It was eerie. No-one was saying anything as we just walked out and I've never liked being anywhere near big crowds ever since.

At my first board meeting at Town I met my fellow board members for the first time – Keith Longbottom was an accountant, Charles

Hodkinson a lawyer, Geoff Headey was a businessman and Leslie Thewlis, a lawyer and absolute gent who was involved in hospital radio and was the most supportive of my plans from the beginning.

The commercial director was Keith Hanvey who was a former player, there was a builder called Brian who helped with repairs around the ground and the final two board members were manager Eoin Hand and club secretary George Binns.

There was a running joke that George could write the minutes up four hours before the meeting he was so efficient.

Turns out I'd been unfair to suggest the board didn't know what they were doing. They had a tough job to do just to keep the club afloat and several had made personal guarantees on bank loans, which is always risky but shows the lengths they'd go to try to preserve the club.

They had somehow kept the club going on the tightest of budgets for 15 years, thanks to Keith's accountancy skills. In short, they'd run it on a shoestring.

After the meeting I asked why Eoin's seat was next to the door in the boardroom and his name was written in chalk on the manager's door.

"That's because managers don't tend to last long here," came the reply.

There were things about the club that immediately concerned me.

Huddersfield Town was formed on August 15, 1908, at the Albert Hotel in Huddersfield town centre and for 80 years had been run like a gentlemen's club to such an extent that no women were allowed in the boardroom at any time and on match days the wives and girlfriends of Huddersfield Town board members and those from the opposing team were herded into another room referred to as 'the hen hutch'.

It's clear head groundsman Ray Chappell loved his pitch with a passion to such an extent no-one was allowed on it – not even the players. He'd banned them from training on it so, in effect, playing at home was like playing away for them, especially new players.

I once organised a training session on the pitch and Ray was so incensed he phoned the chairman to order me off.

That had to change as the pitch at Town was convex so it was quite raised in the middle. This meant that when Eoin peered from his dugout, he couldn't see part of his players' legs on the other side of the pitch.

It also meant it was vital for them to train on the pitch to get used to the curve and turn it to their advantage over the opposition. In the end Ray had to reluctantly agree to the team training on it twice a week, especially when I started to pay the bills to hold the bank off calling in personal guarantees from other board members.

Keith Hanvey was a very well-respected former player and was trying to make Town a commercial success and was the first to moot the idea of building a new stadium.

But he felt he was getting nowhere with the board at the time so left in frustration and went to help Bradford City build a new stand as chief commercial executive before becoming commercial manager at Leeds United.

Like Keith, I was unhappy with the Leeds Road stadium. The toilets were a disgrace – brick-built outbuildings with a trough at foot level and some were even open air. The word 'disgusting' would be a positive description of them.

I think there was just one set of women's toilets in the main stand.

But the final straw was the board meeting when George Binns said £10,000 was needed to repair The Cowshed roof which was falling to bits. The Cowshed was the Town faithful's strongpoint behind one of the goals. It had become so unsafe it had to be closed to protect the fans. There was an awkward silence at the meeting due to the club's financial plight and the decision was deferred.

It was the beginning of the end for the old Leeds Road stadium and the start of a new future.

The board saw the cowshed roof as a disaster. I saw it as an opportunity. An opportunity to think big and go for a new stadium. What was the point trying to maintain a crumbling old ground?

The Taylor Report on the Hillsborough disaster had just come out too and all-seater stadiums were the way forward.

I decided Town must have the first purpose-built all-seater stadium in the UK. Safety had to come first and the old Town ground was crumbling so I set about my quest to build one that would attract the right investors, good footballers, family supporters and staff. It was also to be something for the entire community and set a whole new standard in stadium construction.

It was to be a far rockier road than I could ever have imagined.

I was virtually laughed at by everyone at the club – especially as it was about £700,000 in debt at the time – and that's when everyone's different agendas came to the fore.

The manager wanted money for new players, Keith Longbottom

and George Binns wanted to make the old ground safe in the aftermath of the Bradford City fire in 1985, which claimed 56 lives and left more than 265 injured, Ray Chappell wanted more money for his hallowed turf and, although commercial revenue was growing, it needed taking to another level.

Several first division clubs had built new stands at their grounds but no-one had built a new ground from scratch. To my mind it was the only way forward.

I needed a new commercial manager and former Town striker Steve Kindon recommended ex Burnley and Bolton striker Paul Fletcher who was running the commercial side at Colne Dynamoes FC.

He impressed at the interview and I asked him to bring his wife and children across to my house in Honley the next weekend to meet them before I agreed his contract.

He was puzzled why his family needed to be involved, but I then revealed my full plans, saying: "I'm not just interviewing you as commercial manager for Town, I'm interviewing you to become the chief executive of the first all-seater stadium in the country. It's going to be tough so I need someone loyal and committed 24/7 to the job which is why your family strength is so important. You're going to need that support."

We immediately set about making the club far sounder commercially, connecting it more closely with its sponsors and fans.

Huddersfield Town – directors, players, staff and fans – all had to move in the same direction if we were to achieve the impossible of a new stadium and this was the start, pulling everyone together. In the old days the directors weren't allowed in the dressing room and the players never went in the boardroom.

The change began.

Gola became the new shirt sponsors with some new, striking designs such as a vibrant one with a black and red flash which gave a visual presence that the club was moving in a new, proactive direction.

We gave sponsors and VIPs a free lunch at the Huddersfield Hotel – home of the legendary Johnnys nightclub – with brothers Joe and Johnny Marsden who ran it keen to support us.

Then it was on to the ground where we had converted a spare room into one where sponsors and VIPs could meet injured or reserve players before the match and even the manager popped up for a quick meet and greet around 90 minutes before kick-off.

There were tours of the ground so people could see backstage in the dressing rooms and the boardroom featuring the magnificent trophy Town won for clinching the First Division title three times in a row from 1923 to 1926 under Herbert Chapman – the first club to do so.

Town's other legendary manager was Bill Shankly who probably started his boot room ethos at Town in the late 1950s. The boot room was the place where apprentices would clean the players' boots and learn so much from the first-teamers, but it was also where Shankly would meet in secret with coaches to discuss tactics with the smell of the leather boots in their nostrils.

By the 1990s the 'boot room' was widely credited with Liverpool's amazing success in the 1970s and 1980s. It was a great opportunity to recreate this atmosphere at Town and open it up to the public, so we created the boot room experience.

This was basically the chance for fans to have drinks and food – I think it was no more than sandwiches – in the room that really was the boot room the rest of the week, so it needed a good clean on Fridays ready for match days. Even so, the smell of liniment was always in the air. It was small, pokey, but what an experience which anyone who had been in there would always remember and it brought the supporters closer to their club.

Mind you, if Shankly had remained at Town the club's history could have been so different. Would Huddersfield have become what Liverpool became under Shankly?

He'd brought Denis Law to the club as a 16-year-old, but in December 1957 the board turned down his request for money to buy Ian St John and Ron Yeats. It was the beginning of the end for Shankly who later quit in frustration in 1959, went to manage Liverpool who, like Town, were in the second division and he then signed Ian and Ron.

Liverpool's success rocketed to league titles, FA Cup wins and a UEFA Cup triumph under Shankly, laying the foundations for Liverpool to become European champions for the first time in 1977 while Town ended up in the fourth division.

This had happened because Town lacked ambition, weren't prepared to spend money or take a chance.

We were now in the early 1990s and at another crossroads in Town's fortunes. If we didn't build a new stadium what would Town's fortunes have been bumping along in an old decaying stadium that had mirrored what the club had become – one that continually struggled to make ends meet in a place that was clearly no longer fit for purpose.

We needed support to make it happen and so I looked to Kirklees Council.

The leader at the time was John Harman and he invited me to his office in Huddersfield Town Hall and I felt nervous walking up the steps.

He was in the office he shared with his deputy Dave Harris who was sitting with his feet on the desk drinking beer.

Dave was initially dismissive of the idea saying we hadn't a "hope in hell" of building a new stadium with the club stuck in the third division, but John took a more considered approach and certainly didn't dismiss it out of hand. He knew the importance of the club to the town.

Over time I became friends with Dave and John who became one of the new stadium's most powerful advocates and supporters.

So much so that without him we couldn't have done it. After all, Kirklees owned the land where the old Leeds Road stadium stood and the club had signed a new 125-year lease with the council just three years before.

Why the stadium had to be more than just a football arena

The stadium had become my field of dreams with the ethos that if you build it, people will come.

Don't forget that at that time Huddersfield Town were towards the bottom of the old third division with average crowds of around 5,000. The town's rugby team, known affectionately as Fartown where their crumbling ground was based, had only 2,000 or so and that was on a good day.

We wanted to build a stadium for around 25,000 fans which was another reason for folk laughing at us every time we mentioned it.

But, in life, you have to be a visionary and succeed. This was one of those times. We weren't just thinking of the here and now, we were looking to a brighter future.

Yet at the heart of all this it had to make financial sense too and I wanted to pay back everything we'd need to borrow to build the stadium in three to five years. That was always my business model at Galpharm – pay back in a strict timetable – and I wanted the same for the stadium.

First of all we needed a proper commercial plan to be sure it could be done before we even set off on our journey.

We were introduced to Tony Stephens who went on to become David Beckham's agent and had great insights into the football industry. He drew up an incredibly in-depth commercial report looking at every way the new stadium could make money and what other clubs had done to improve their grounds. My brief to him was, 'What would make money in a brand new all-seater stadium?'

One thing quickly became obvious. Although clubs had built stands, no-one had built a new stadium for donkey's years and ours would be the first ever all-seater stadium in the UK.

In the aftermath of the Hillsborough disaster in April 1989 and the Taylor report published in January 1990, all first and second division clubs would have to become all-seater. If Town had been promoted they would have had to convert Leeds Road and the cost would have been astronomical. Seats couldn't have been fixed to the terracing as it was. The stands would have had to be gutted and rebuilt.

The old Fartown ground was also crumbling away – its heyday had been the interwar years – and everything was now wrong about the place from the state of the stadium and its access to the perilous state of the club's finances.

There really was no choice. Huddersfield had to have a new stadium for the modern era that both clubs could share to make it viable and sustainable. To me there was absolutely no other option and to have tried to stay at Leeds Road would have been madness in the long term.

We started to look for potential sites and thought about the stadium well out of town near the M62, but there was no suitable land available and Kirklees Council leader John Harman then suggested the land just across the river from the Leeds Road stadium and which had been an old tip.

It was tough trying to get support from several local councillors. They regarded football and rugby as sports run by what they thought were elitist boards with small crowds compared to the number of people living in Kirklees and so should pay their own way with the council not getting involved.

Fortunately, wiser heads guided by Cllr Harman realised the significance of successful football and rugby clubs to the town, its heritage and even its morale. Fast forward 25 years and the new stadium was sold out every week when Huddersfield Town gained promotion to the Premier League and the rugby team had been completely refreshed as Huddersfield Giants thanks to chairman Ken Davy and his wife Jennifer, often doing well in its league and reaching the Challenge Cup final in May 2022 where they lost to Wigan Warriors by just a couple of points. The feelgood factor in the town when its sports teams are doing well is palpable. Even non-sports fans can feel the positivity.

A new stadium would mean one arena, one community, one focal point for all the town's major events. It was essential to me to deliver a profitable, sustainable and totally independent financial company – Kirklees Stadium Development Ltd – for both the stadium's tenants and the wider community.

It also meant the stadium had to be independent which was why Kirklees Stadium Development Ltd was set up.

We knew, though, it couldn't be all done at once if we stuck to my initial plan. The initial costs for the stadium would be £10.8m – a mixture of money from the sale of the old ground along with a grant from the Football Trust and the rest borrowed from the banks underwritten by the council. That would only pay for the two main stands, the pitch and car park so the stadium would be short of the two ends in the early years until they could be afforded. The two main stands could take up to 10,000 people so would be big enough for the kind of crowds the teams were attracting in those days.

We were also the stadium pioneers so could sell our designs and marketing plans to other clubs following in our footsteps. We'd done all the groundwork so they wouldn't have to start from scratch. That legacy lives on to today as I've recently been approached to advise on developing The Shay stadium in Halifax.

The Huddersfield stadium would be more than home for football and rugby. It needed to be an entertainment complex that made a profit so the plans included a banqueting suite, function rooms and office space along with a neighbouring cinema and pub to lease and a creche to help working families.

We also wanted to include bedrooms inside the stadium too which could be transformed into corporate boxes on match days with the beds folding away into the walls. After all, the pitch is the hallowed turf in all stadiums and who wouldn't want to wake up to that view.

As it turns out, the banqueting suite is the biggest space of its kind in Huddersfield for countless functions from awards and exhibitions to fundraising charity dinners and still is today. Everyone knows it and has probably been to an event there.

More and more people were starting to play golf but Huddersfield didn't have a driving range so that became part of the plan too. Others disagreed and said it should be a ski slope but I didn't think that would make as much money for the stadium.

I even included two wind turbines on the nearby banking to help power the stadium and any excess could be sold back to the grid. That was in the very earliest days of wind turbine technology when I think there was only one in Huddersfield, helping to power the famous Longley Farm dairy cream and yoghurt manufacturers at Holmfirth.

We needed to be sure we were going down the right track with the stadium design and one option would have been to look at other stadiums in the lower English football league divisions but that never remotely crossed my mind.

I thought big right from the start and don't forget that in those days you couldn't just Google stadiums to look at lots of different options online in an hour or so.

I've relatives in Canada who told me about their fantastic new stadium the Toronto SkyDome (now known as the Rogers Centre) which had opened in June 1989 with far more than sport in mind.

So I travelled to Canada with Paul Fletcher to see it for ourselves. Yes, it was home to the Toronto Blue Jays baseball team but the down-to-earth architect Rod Robbie – a Scottish guy we met who wore a trademark donkey jacket and looked more like a labourer than a stadium designer – had been visionary and was still over there.

Our bedrooms were in the 50,000-seater stadium, it had a retractable roof which alone cost $250m and was sponsored by Coca-Cola. The stadium had cost $600m dollars and had a Hard Rock Café inside. It would be the place for music concerts and all kinds of events – even classic cars. The local authority had invested about $250m into it knowing that in the decades to come it would bring hundreds of millions of dollars into the local economy. It's worked, with Taylor Swift due to play six concerts there in November 2024.

The Toronto SkyDome was a blueprint for the future which we needed to see in action so we could take the affordable parts of their concept and work it into ours.

We came back enthused and exhilarated, raring to go knowing that what we were doing was not only right but the only way forward for Huddersfield and its sports teams.

In our first pitch to the council they turned us down flat with one councillor saying the stadium must have a running track inside. That would never have worked. A track would only be used a handful of times a year and the distance it would put between the players and the fans would wreck the atmosphere.

Paul was disillusioned with the decision and was even thinking of walking away, but we sat down in one of Huddersfield's famous Merrie England coffee shops and in its old mock Tudor surroundings I convinced Paul that the stadium plan must and would work and that we'd get there in the end.

There was so much financial potential with the new stadium getting rent money from the football and rugby teams plus other sports events such as the Rugby World Cup and rock concerts, food and drink on sale on match days on its concourses, events in the banqueting suite, sponsorship for the ground and its individual stands, rent from office space and leases from pub and cinema companies for the pub and multi-screen cinema on site and money from the creche.

In the 1970s and 80s you'd be lucky to get a pie and a cup of Bovril at Town. Now there would be every reason for fans to get there early and soak up the atmosphere rather than arriving 15 minutes before kick-off with long queues at the turnstiles.

It was suddenly starting to sound achievable. The construction company, McAlpine, needed a showcase to get contracts for other stadiums and ours was that showcase which meant the McAlpine quote was very reasonable and made it affordable.

The whole scheme would be underwritten by Kirklees Council and with grants from the Sports Council and the rest in loans there was every chance any money borrowed would have been paid back within my five-year timetable.

The next vital step was to appoint an architect and we had interest from six practices. The main clue I gave them to what I wanted was to draw a big heart on the ordnance survey map indicating the stadium was to be the heart of the community.

Up to then football and rugby stadiums were used for half a day once a fortnight and just nine months of the year. We needed someone who could think a long way outside those boxes.

We didn't want it to look anything like a box, either.

Architect Rod Sheard from the Lobb Partnership was the only one who phoned me up and asked if this meant the design shouldn't conform to the normal. I simply replied, "I couldn't possibly comment," in case it was misconstrued as giving too much information, but Rod instantly knew from the tone of my voice his design not only had to be out of the ordinary, it had to be extraordinary.

He'd already had some experience with stadiums, designing the West Stand funded by Sir Elton John at Watford in 1986 and the South Stand at Twickenham.

When his initial designs came through it got everyone's pulses racing and blood flowing. We thought, 'Wow, this guy absolutely gets what we are trying to achieve here.'

It was visionary in an age when designs weren't computer-generated. The arc beams were there to make sure everyone in the stadium got a panoramic view. It was a real field of dreams here in Yorkshire ... and for a club languishing in the third division. Now that is a dream!

Rod later wrote a book called *Sports Architecture* which goes into detail about the challenging technical issues around constructing sports buildings and features Huddersfield's stadium along with some of the best stadiums around the world, including Stadium Australia built in the late 1990s and which has similarities to ours.

Getting the planning permission was also complex but that was steered through by Huddersfield planning consultant Paul Sykes from SPBS Planning Services no matter how choppy the waters got during the process. He was our eyes and ears when it came to all things planning and we trusted Paul 100% to get the job done, which he did.

We needed Sports Council money so we had a scale 6ft by 4ft model made which we took to the House of Commons to show the world. We needed a big stage for such a big project. If we'd launched it in Huddersfield town hall then no-one would have come. We took it to the seat of power so it wasn't just on their doorstep, it was actually inside their dining room so everyone we wanted to see it in the so-called 'corridors of power' would get the chance to do so.

Everyone who looked at the design was enthralled by it. We knew there was no turning back now. The momentum was starting and we just needed to keep driving it forward.

I then held a fans' forum in Huddersfield town hall to explain our vision to the Town faithful. The fact we needed the town hall says it all really. The only place we could have done it at the old Leeds Road stadium was the Greenall Suite, but that would have been way too small.

Once the news was out the backlash started with fans coming up to me on the street, in pubs and restaurants, with most of them berating me saying that Town needed to spend money on players, not a stadium. Things got so bad I stopped going out in Huddersfield and my family and I started travelling to Leeds or Manchester just to get a night out in peace.

To try to keep things going for the club financially we launched a share option and a weekly lottery and I wrote a piece for the programme in March 1993 which pulled no punches, revealing that directors past and present had ploughed £1.4m into the club and urged the fans to rally round and support us by doing the lottery or buying shares.

I warned them the club's survival depended on it and said quite starkly: "Please help us to ensure we survive in the football league. Since taking over as chairman my main task has been to tackle the £1m debt that has accumulated in the short term and steps have already been taken to keep us alive.

"Crowds of 9,500 and 10,000 are needed now to break even. We have to face reality and, while we are accelerating things as quickly as possible, it is hard for us to afford signings at the moment.

"Some supporters believe, wrongly, that we are allowing the club to slip towards relegation while the new stadium takes top priority. Funding is totally separate and the club's finances are not being drained by the project. Neither can we utilise any funding in the stadium for the football club's benefit.

"Only when we have independent profits coming in from first-class facilities will we be able to build a team of players on a more secure basis. If we don't plan ahead for regular, fresh cash coming into the club then there won't be a football club in a few years' time.

"That's why the new stadium project is the key to our future."

Having said all that, hardly anyone supported the idea and even some of my closest friends thought I'd lost the plot with this one.

But the finances were coming together with £2m from the sale of the old Leeds Road to be turned into a retail park, £2m from the Sports Foundation and the rest borrowed with a financial plan starting to be plotted out.

But storm clouds were looming over Leeds Road with the potential to scupper everything.

Town gets a reluctant new chairman ... me

Huddersfield Town had been operating in debt for years and which had been slowly getting worse.

The directors had done all they could to keep the club going to the point that several of them had personal guarantees with the bank, which meant that if the bank ever called 'time' on the loans they would have to pay up. This would have a devastating impact on their lives, especially as some had pledged six-figure sums.

The team, managed by Ian Ross, was struggling on the pitch and on December 19, 1992, lost 2–0 at home to Chester City leaving them three points adrift at the bottom of Division Two and staring relegation in the face.

Hundreds of passionate Town fans were waiting outside to have a go at chairman Keith Longbottom, even though he'd kept it going for the best part of 20 years against all odds. He decided enough was enough and quit, handing me the poisoned chalice of the chairmanship at the age of 46 as no-one else wanted it. Most of the board left with him.

The Huddersfield Examiner commented at the time: "It is not only the personnel but, more importantly, the personality of the club which has changed."

Myself and my accountant at Galpharm, Melvyn Hoyle, went into the club to go over the books. It was supposed to be for a few hours and we ended up there for three days and two nights – even sleeping at the stadium – trying to unravel and understand the finances.

We discovered the club was in a perilous financial position and we'd just gone into the New Year when the bank, Lloyds, looked to foreclose on the loans which meant those who had given personal guarantees faced financial catastrophe. If they didn't have the cash, the bank would take their homes, businesses or other assets. At that time directors thought football clubs would never go bust, but Town was in grave danger of proving that theory very wrong.

I just couldn't let that happen. Huddersfield was way too big a town to not have professional football and rugby clubs, so I pleaded with the bank to give me more time and also mentioned that if they bust the club I would make sure the people of Huddersfield would never forgive them and they'd be the first bank to have put an English league club out of business.

The main problem at Town was that the income stream was so limited – mainly just through the turnstiles – but we now had a vision for the future. We had to somehow get through the next few months and the only way was for me to put hundreds of thousands of pounds in to keep it going.

The bank gave me four months and in that time my aim was to bring new people into the boardroom with fresh funding, come up with a financial plan to show we were in control and explain how a new stadium would be making a profit within three or four years.

Looking back, I think that era cost my company Galpharm almost £5m because I was so focused on saving Town and building a new stadium rather than my own business. There was also a heavy personal cost as it ruined my second marriage to Ann. I was just never at home to support my wife and children, Alex and Fay.

But things then suddenly took a serious turn for the worse for me.

On Boxing Day a charity football match was organised at Marsden, a village near Huddersfield on the main road to Manchester.

It was set up by former Town and England star Trevor Cherry who I'd brought into the club to drive our young player recruitment forward. He was very highly respected in Yorkshire so was ideal to attract young talent to Town.

I was playing at right back but somehow found myself in the rare position of charging through with the ball so that I was one-on-one with the goalie who I seem to recall was former Manchester City number one, the legendary Joe Corrigan, as he was Town's goalkeeping coach at the time.

There was a massive bang and the next thing I remember I was lying on the touchline. It turns out Joe had blocked me and taken me totally out of the game. I came round concussed and in severe pain all down my left side. Over the coming days and weeks the bruising came out – I was black, blue and all kinds of other colours too.

Even though I was in terrible pain I managed to chair the annual general meeting in February 1993 when it was revealed Town had made a loss of £365,000. The previous year the loss was £367,000 and the year before that £84,000.

I'd loaned the club £135,000 even though I only took £28,000 in salary from Galpharm in 1992 and it was only years later I discovered my loan was twice the amount of what anyone else had put in. The players' salaries were £8,500 a week with staff and other costs amounting to a further £7,500 a week.

I managed to attract some new board members including Terry Fisher who owned local travel agency Travelworld and brought some money into the club, accountant David Taylor and businessman Malcolm Asquith. I even walked out on to the pitch one match day with a microphone and asked if anyone in the crowd wanted to invest in the club. No-one came forward.

The serious threat of administration and possibly the end for Town continually hung over the club, but we just needed to keep going until the new stadium could be built and the February AGM had brought it all into sharp focus.

I'd sorted out the business model and commercial plans for the stadium – all the ways it would make money and be profitable – appointed a world-leading architect and McAlpine were on board as the construction company.

We really needed to get moving with it – every month was vital by this stage – so on March 3 at my home in Honley everyone signed up to the agreement that the stadium would be built and be shared by the football and rugby league clubs. I was chairman of both Town and the Kirklees Stadium Development Company so I signed for both, Kirklees leader Cllr John Harman signed for the council and Fartown chairman Joe Bramley for the rugby league club.

After long negotiations we had finally agreed that the council and Huddersfield Town would each have a 40% share in the stadium with the rugby league club 20%.

The moment it was signed I felt a huge sense of relief – it was almost as though all the pressure drained from my body and the pain took over again. I left the room and went straight to bed leaving Cllr Harman to finish the meeting.

The football injury had taken a severe toll on my body and I was paralysed for four to five weeks. My whole left side had seized up suffering from muscle spasms, nerves had become trapped, I often had to wear a neck brace and was spending a lot of time in bed trying to recover.

It was a strange time. No-one from Huddersfield Town's Board came to see me, although George Binns did. He had left his role as Town secretary by then and I'd brought him in to work on the stadium to deal with all the legal requirements and administration needed to fast-track the stadium and get it built so quickly.

Apparently rumours began to circulate that I was suffering from a mental illness. Well, I was taking exceptionally strong painkillers which, apparently, could send you doolally. Someone even claimed they'd seen me walking about outside in my pyjamas which seemed very strange as I don't wear pyjamas.

I was told that Terry Fisher was running the football club with Paul Fletcher heading up the stadium.

Something made me decide to do a check on Companies House and I discovered that I'd resigned as chairman of both KSDL and Huddersfield Town on March 13, 1993. I was totally shocked. I hadn't signed any documents – it was a physical impossibility as I was half paralysed in bed at the time.

I went to the July board meeting to find out what was going on and was told changes had had to be made because I was ill. All I can say is these changes weren't with my consent. I'd gone to this board meeting ready to carry on as chairman. Instead, they offered me the presidency of Huddersfield Town AFC … but only for a year.

I turned it down and said I wanted some of the money I'd loaned to the club back within a week. Highly experienced solicitor Gerald Jarvis, senior partner at top Huddersfield commercial law firm Baxter Caulfield, made this happen for me quickly.

My accountant Melvyn Hoyle also set up a company called Huddersfield Town Football Club Ltd to protect my interests and I became the sole shareholder. It has one share worth £1.

I left the club, hurt and deeply disappointed about the way I'd been treated.

Not one director from Huddersfield Town AFC contacted me again and I wasn't even invited to the opening of the new stadium. Having been the founder chairman and creator of the stadium development company that really hurt and was the deepest cut of all.

I'd been Town chairman for 69 days – the shortest reign in the club's history. I contend to this day that if I'd remained chairman of KSDL and Town the stadium would not have ended up burdened with debt as it still is today and causing problems for the new Town owner Kevin Nagle in 2024.

It would have been debt-free quickly but decisions were made to borrow more and more to get both stadium ends done, a swimming pool and Kirklees Council offices built and that's why the stadium continues to be a financial liability for anyone thinking of taking it on.

Why I just had to have the Galpharm name on the first ever purpose-built all-seater stadium in the UK

I'd moved heaven and earth to get the stadium built but for the first 10 years it bore the name of the construction company, McAlpine.

By 2004 it needed a new sponsor but it seemed no-one was coming forward so there was a danger it would remain nameless or, even worse, be known as Kirklees Stadium. Kirklees is a made-up name stretching back to 1974 for the municipal council covering a huge area of West Yorkshire that includes both Huddersfield and Dewsbury. To put it mildly, the name's not universally liked or recognised so I thought I'd step in.

Galpharm had never spent a penny on advertising. Our marketing strategy was our price which beat everyone else. People could see that immediately they walked into the pharmacies and shops.

But now I was thinking bigger and you don't get much bigger than a stadium. We had a board meeting at Galpharm headquarters and I'd flown in specially from Gibraltar to attend. The sponsorship deal was £75,000 a year making it £750,000 for 10 years. A bargain in sponsorship terms, especially when you think of the millions it now costs companies just to get their names on teams' shirts.

Not everyone was in favour but I argued the case, said I had a plane to catch back to Gibraltar, got up and left.

Someone asked if a decision had been made as no-one seemed to have agreed. Craig put them straight.

"Dad's decided," he said. "The name's going on the stadium."

And it did, getting us global recognition with the football, rugby and rock concerts and was also on road and motorway signs. I think it also meant a lot to Huddersfield Town fans too as it had such local connotations and it's a kind of warm name that trips off the tongue and is still affectionately referred to as 'The Pharm'. Many folk still don't realise GAL stands for my names Graham Andrew Leslie, but there you go.

Within a few weeks I think everyone at Galpharm understood the vision and the workforce was clearly so proud the stadium was named after the company where they worked. It lifted spirits and helped to make us one big family – including the thousands who manufactured for us overseas.

I also insisted in the agreement that whoever bought Galpharm from me honoured the deal for the full 10 years … and they did.

The stadium broke all the conventions of stadium design and led the way for so many other stadium designs and, ultimately, the new Wembley.

It captured the imagination of architects worldwide and in 1995, the year after it opened, the stadium was named the Royal Institute of British Architects (RIBA) Building of the Year and remains the only sports stadium to ever win the UK's top architectural prize.

The lead designer was Rod Sheard from global architects Populous and on their website, site architect for the project Dale Jennins says: "Before this project I don't think big-name architects would have been interested in designing stadiums. They were seen as just these crinkly tin sheds built for containing people. But the John Smith's changed all of that."

A section on the Populous website about the stadium says: "The John Smith's Stadium broke all the conventions of a football stadium as a cold, unwelcoming building offering little more than a plastic cup of tea and a pie on a dingy corridor.

"It was a deliberate policy of Populous's interior design team to use a variety of vibrant colours throughout the building. Where other architects may have used solid walls around the lifts and stairs, Populous used glass blocks, trimmed in the blue and white of the town's football colours, to offer visibility and uplift.

"As one of the earliest examples of a multi-use stadium to be shared by two professional clubs playing different sports, part of the brief called for the co-occupiers of the venue to be able to function as independently as possible.

"This is reflected in the distribution of permanent accommodation for each party. Club offices with their own private entrances and dedicated entertainment areas help establish a sense of identity in a shared venue. These facilities created new opportunities for revenue generation on non-match days – a relatively novel concept at the time, but one that has become the bedrock of modern business planning for stadiums."

The stadium was needed because Lord Justice Taylor's report into the Hillsborough Disaster recommended that all grounds in the old first and second divisions – now the Premier League and Football

League Championship – should be all-seater by August 1994 and that clubs in the former third and fourth divisions – the current leagues 1 and 2 – should be all-seater by August 1999. We achieved that timetable with the stadium opening in August 1994 which was all the more incredible when you think the contract to build the stadium was only signed in March 1993.

Once more we were ahead of the curve.

It would have been virtually impossible to turn the old Leeds Road into an all-seater stadium and far more economical to simply build a new one that looked to a brighter future for both the football and rugby clubs and the town.

Up to then most grounds were built like boxes with supporting columns that partially blocked the view. The new stadium used new design technology based on the curved roof trusses to make sure that everyone in the ground had a full and uninterrupted view from every seat.

It broke conventions and set a new standard and aspirations for what stadiums should look like – striking, modern, landmark buildings – and the facilities it should provide to create revenue on non-match days.

This was pioneering at the time but is now the starting point when new stadiums are designed and built.

My tips on how to do well in business

Contacts are vital in business and you can quickly improve yours by playing a simple game I call Leslie Links.

If you're with a business colleague or someone you know is well connected, both get your phones out and start scrolling down your contacts starting with A and revealing who is in your contacts book.

It's amazing how many connections other people have that could be vital to your own business and so sharing a few opens up new horizons – and potentially doors – for both of you.

It turns out that people you know often have contacts you've been trying to reach for ages but never managed to get through to them.

Well, the key to that contact may be sitting in the same room as you but you'll never know unless you get your phones out.

In the 1980s and 90s most of our medicines were being manufactured in India but there was a problem in the monsoon season from June to September.

The sheer humidity was making our aspirin from India become unstable – in short, the moisture was causing it to start to disintegrate in the packaging. All the other medicines were fine, it was just the aspirin.

This meant we needed to source a new supplier in a different part of the world and we discovered a potential manufacturer in China, so I flew over with Richard Eggleston, head of research and development at Galpharm, and my future wife Karen to speak to the boss and, hopefully, come back with a deal.

It turned out they were a massive pharmaceutical company and when we walked into the boardroom there was Richard and I on one side of the table and six representatives of their company on the other.

I got up and moved my chair to the head of the table next to where their chief executive would sit when he arrived. His six representatives seemed surprised but said nothing. When the chief executive walked in a few minutes later he immediately spotted I'd been rearranging his boardroom with my chair next to his.

I said I hoped he didn't mind but, as we were about to forge a partnership, we should sit together at the head of the table. He smiled, sat down and we got started, but after a day and a half of tough negotiating we were still struggling to strike a deal we were both happy with as the volumes we needed were a tiny fraction of their output.

I stood up, walked to the window, looked out and spotted a stream with a willow tree next to it. I was instantly inspired to go down a different tack.

I turned round, looked the company chief executive straight in the face and said to him: "You can't refuse to supply us with aspirin."

He looked puzzled and asked why.

I replied: "Because you're the home of aspirin. There is a willow tree out there and thousands of years before Christ was born a poultice was made from willow bark as a pain reliever for Chinese soldiers injured in battle."

The boss looked out of the window, stared at the willow and then turned and said: "You're right. After that reminder I can't refuse you."

If I'd never gone to China and had that moment of inspiration looking out of the window at nature we'd never have secured the deal. The thought was a trigger point and then it's a matter of having the cheek to carry it through but by that stage we had everything to gain and nothing to lose. It just shows you have to be there to spot those moments and make the most of them.

Here's another one to make colleagues stop and think out of the box.

Give them a paper clip and ask them what they can do with it – what can it be used for? People normally start with four or five ideas.

Then open it out so part of it stands up on a desk and ask again. They come up with more ideas.

Open it out fully or bend it at a right angle and people suddenly see even more new uses for it.

This is all about mindset and creativity. Don't look at things – or, indeed, life in general – in a one-dimensional way. Always look to think creatively, differently and out of the box.

Yes, always be focused, be driven but never let yourself be limited or restricted. Those who succeed tend to have a vision, a sense of creativity and the determination to deliver that vision no matter what obstacles are thrown in their way.

I always have a paper clip on my desk to remind me to do that.

Loving helping businesses ... but sometimes it doesn't quite work out

I'm sometimes described as a business mentor but I'm not keen on that word as I think it can sound a bit patronising.

I'm now known as a business coach. I advise and do my best to keep companies on track because once they veer off course, even slightly by just one degree, then things can ultimately go very wrong.

I'm a big believer in the Pareto Theory which states that 80% of consequences come from 20% of causes. In a commercial sense I think the figures are slightly different but, in short, 70% of your business and profit normally comes from just 30% of your customers.

This is the same for just about any business you could think of from hairdressing to retail, building firms to holiday companies and whether your sales are £60,000 a year or £60m.

To simplify it even more, roughly two-thirds of your business success relies on a third of your customers. The trick then is to improve your sales and marketing so the ratio improves and you're less reliant on those 30% of customers.

After all, that 30% could quickly diminish along with your business with those loyal customers perhaps moving to another part of the country, being tempted away by your competitors, having less to spend or, sadly, even dying.

Businesses do anything they can think of to increase that 30% including discounts, loyalty cards and special offers through to more subtle ways such as Next which rotates its stock every few weeks rather than every season to keep enticing its customers back in through the doors to see what's new. By doing so you only need a few loyal customers and you don't have to spend fortunes enticing new ones through the doors.

Think as a customer, not as a seller. What does the customer want from you and why? For most middle-income earners it's good quality and consistency at the right price. They also want it to be an experience so make sure customer service is spot on, not just paying lip service. The customer knows when it's genuine and when it's fake and just going through the motions. Give it emotion instead.

When it comes to business, real success often only comes after several failures and I can think of a couple from my time at the university. These were businesses that sounded really promising but, in the end, didn't work out.

One was called Renal Freedom and was devised by a Huddersfield University student on kidney dialysis. He had the idea for a portable dialysis device so people could go on holidays and weekends away rather than being stuck on machines in hospitals or at home.

I helped him to put together a business plan and model but advised him that his biggest problem would be taking on a market dominated by a giant American multinational company called Baxter Healthcare which specialised in treating kidney conditions.

I suggested he should offer them the chance to buy his product but he wanted to go it alone and do it independently.

He took his idea to a trade show for renal products in Blackpool and because he couldn't afford a stand I gave him a crafty tip to make sure everyone at the show noticed him and wanted to find out more. I arranged for someone with a video camera to follow him everywhere he went in the show, giving the impression a documentary was being made about him and everyone would want to know who he was, what he was doing and why.

One lead he got from this sounded promising at first. A guy from America wanted to meet him to find out more but I insisted I was at the meeting, which was held in Huddersfield, ironically at the stadium.

Turns out he had Huddersfield connections, knew who I was and was shocked to see me there. Caught by surprise, he eventually admitted he was trying to steal the idea and sell it in America and was after every bit of information he could get about the product.

Luckily we'd rumbled him and sent him packing back to the good old US of A. Turns out his business consisted of 22 researchers who spent their days looking at recent patents globally, researching the companies who had made the applications and then looking for an Achilles heel to exploit. It may be they were underfunded or running low on cash and so were vulnerable to these commercial vultures.

They knew that if they stole the idea, copied it and released it in America the original company would never be able to afford to pursue them through the courts over there.

The story has a happy ending though. The young man's kidney repaired itself, he didn't need dialysis anymore and his interest in pursuing this business idea waned.

His health was more important than any business venture.

Sometimes in business you can get carried away.

I went on a trip to buy a flat in Torremolinos and met with a car dealer from Huddersfield, Lou Lomax, who was also interested in buying one in the same block. I'd never met him before so he wore a black suit, white shirt and a white carnation so I'd spot him at the airport.

The night we arrived England were knocked out of the 1982 World Cup after a 0–0 draw with hosts Spain, so we drowned our sorrows and were a little worse for wear when we went to look at the apartments and we both chose penthouses. We were asked to sign several documents for a Spanish bank which had taken over the apartments after the builder had ceased trading.

It was only later we realised we'd actually bought the entire block of 65 apartments. We thought about trying to sell them and even approached people on the beach the next day to see if they wanted to buy an apartment, but then flew home wondering how on earth we'd ever pay for them.

I phoned my lawyer, explained the situation and how buying the entire block had all been a big mix-up. He contacted the Spanish bank, said it had been a confusing misunderstanding, explained we didn't have the money to fulfil the contract, but said that as a gesture of goodwill we'd buy two apartments each which we did to get us off the hook.

I sold mine a few years later and ploughed the money into Galpharm.

It just shows you need to make sure you read everything before signing and fully understand it, even if it's in a foreign language. Especially if it's in a foreign language.

The tower block is still standing and I pass it every time I drive from Malaga to our home in Spain.

When you're an entrepreneur not everything is successful and, ironically, one of the biggest disappointments was when I got involved in a venture called Let's Save Some Money. It had been set up by entrepreneur Michael Toxvaerd and his wife, Sarah Willingham, who turned The Bombay Bicycle Club into the largest and most successful Indian restaurant chain in the UK and went on to star on *Dragons' Den*.

The concept of Let's Save Some Money was a business that sold advice and money-saving tips to people who signed up, but unfortunately it never took off with money-saving guru Martin Lewis continuing to dominate that market.

Michael and Sarah tried to make it work with joint ventures and forging partnerships but it never achieved the momentum or the hits so, in the end, they called it a day. It was an investment where I'd let my heart rule my head, but I didn't lose too much in the venture and every experience like this is an important learning curve.

The couple have gone on to great success in the hospitality sector which shows that everyone, myself included, will have a blip at some point where a business doesn't take off like you hoped it would.

In 2013 I was invited to speak to an Entrepreneurs Club in Leeds where a young man called Adam Roberts had come up with a concept where people could instantly find out about restaurants in a place they were visiting – restaurants with recommendations and the ability to book them through a one-stop website.

Adam's concept was called Go Dine and he'd started it in Nottingham. With a limited budget he'd cleverly taken on university students to help with the website, IT, administration and social media. The technology was excellent but the operation lacked people to get out there selling the concept.

You can have a brilliant business on paper but it's not a business until it's making money. That's what it's all about, that all-important bottom line.

We gave Go Dine money, time and financial advice but Covid crippled this business sector and stopped it in its tracks.

Another venture had a bizarre start, a promising future and then a big but …

In 2014 I was asked to give a talk to business people at an 8am breakfast event and we were at the point of the breakfast being served when in came a slim entrepreneur in his mid-40s with a natural swagger, blond hair and a cheeky smile.

Being short, fat and hairy I naturally took an instant dislike to him.

He then announced: "Who the hell owns that soft top red Ferrari outside with the registration number G1RLS?"

"That'll be mine," I replied.

"Oh Christ," he said. "It makes my Ferrari look boring."

I then instantly took a liking to him and we got on from that moment.

His name was Julian Wiley and his mission in life was to revolutionise the energy business.

At first this was with wind turbines and he was working with the University of Huddersfield to try to solve a stability problem he had with wind turbines he was importing from China. I loaned him £3m to help him through a short-term cash flow problem and he paid it back with full interest before the due date and also personally reimbursed any customers that had had an issue with their turbines.

Now that's how business should be done.

In 2016 Julian came to me *Dragons' Den*-style to say he was starting another business and did I want to invest around £150,000 for a 10% stake?

It was to set up storage batteries in homes and businesses in the UK so people could power them up during the cheap tariff periods such as in the middle of the night and then use the power from the batteries during the day. In sunny countries the system would use just solar panels and batteries.

"Sounds exciting," I said, knowing very little about the energy sector. "How many have you sold so far?"

"None," replied Julian.

I followed this up with: "What are you going to call this company?"

"Don't know yet," he replied.

Reflecting on his last two answers, I said: "So, just let me recap. You want to sell me 10% of a company with no name, no sales, no product, yet you already value this supposedly unmissable business opportunity at £1.5m."

"Well, yes," he said, kind of exasperated that I hadn't immediately grasped the full significance of what he was offering me here. "It's a once-in-a-lifetime opportunity. Are you in?"

"I suppose so," I replied. So we signed our first shareholders agreement.

He needed a brand that people would know and trust and after a lot of negotiation signed a deal with Duracell and set up a company called Social Energy.

The batteries, by the way, would be quite big at 3ft by 3ft by 1ft so they'd take up a decent amount of storage room in a house.

The concept was based on the idea of grid sharing, with customers mainly using solar panels and batteries that connected them and shared energy.

A chance meeting in a London pub led to an Oxford-based research and development company called Levelise getting involved and which had the technology to get the system up and running.

The project was getting to speedboat pace, with an energy trading company the next necessary purchase and staff trained to get the business actually operating. It was first launched in Australia with cricket legend Shane Warne promoting it, but by now more than 100 investors had become involved. I began to have concerns about the direction the business was taking with pressure piled on me to invest more to maintain a 10% stake and so I resigned and left the board.

Then Covid struck and Social Energy Australia ended up in administration in the backdrop to soaring energy prices so I was right to cut my losses when I did.

In my view it failed due to an over ambitious company valuation – it grew from £1.5m in 2016 to £100m in 2018 – and over ambitious sales targets coupled with a lack of sales and distribution.

Why helping others is in the blood

When you've worked in business all your life there is something in your DNA that keeps driving you forward.

In around 2007 I was invited to be a member of the Government's All-Party Health Select Committee, but only lasted a couple of meetings.

The reason was I was too radical for them. I saw a National Health Service bogged down with far too much management interference and red tape and the impact that had on those working right at the sharp end.

My suggestions included radically streamlining the management structure, harnessing technology more and giving the nurses and doctors more freedom, away from what I regarded as bureaucratic abuse.

I felt the structure was way outdated even to the point that many individual hospital trusts had their own pharmaceutical manufacturing units but only supplied their own hospitals in the trust. If they'd all shared their expertise and made the medications available to one another each trust could have made money and also saved a fortune having to buy more expensive medicines from pharmaceutical companies.

That's how Galpharm ended up saving the NHS many millions of pounds every year and continues to do so, simply by radically cutting the cost of medicines such as paracetamol and ibuprofen.

In many ways the NHS remains an inflexible dinosaur which is why it's lost so many staff in recent years ... staff who would probably go back if there was far less red tape, policies and procedures which deflect them from their core tasks of caring for patients.

During my time on the committee at the House of Commons I met the former Conservative leader William Hague. We got chatting, I told him I'd sold my pharmaceutical business and he remarked that I'd clearly been very successful in one sector of industry.

I think I took that the wrong way as something jarred with me ... the phrase 'one sector'. I got it into my head that I needed success in other areas of business and prove to both myself and, I suppose, William Hague that I was no one-trick pony.

Once Galpharm had gone there was a huge void in my life replaced with a commodity I knew very little about ... money. I knew I wanted to put it to some good helping others. Business is tough and everyone needs a helping hand at some point.

And so it began, my quest to support those starting out in businesses or suddenly finding they were in need of help or guidance. I'd spent decades building up experience and knowledge and now passionately wanted to pass it on to those who would benefit.

One of the first was a Bradford-based commercial photography company called Trafalgar owned by fashion photographer Graham Nelson and artistic director Chris Heeley which had run into trading difficulties during the economic crash. They specialised in taking high quality images of bathrooms, bedrooms and kitchens for all the main retailers such as B&Q, Homebase, Wickes and Magnet.

These were big contracts as Trafalgar needed to rent large amounts of warehouse space, organise to have the kitchens, taps and all the other accessories sent to them from around the world, which was a logistical nightmare, build the kitchens, light them and then take the photos. It was a mammoth, time-consuming task, perhaps building 25 kitchens to put one catalogue together, but that's how they did it back then with the market set to continue expanding.

Then the 2008 economic crash hit and the market collapsed. Trafalgar's owners had no option but to place the business into receivership even though they had an amazing workforce that offered to work just for pizza and beer money in a bid to try to keep the business going. It was an amazing culture to have, a brilliant reflection on the two directors and a strong reason why I wanted to help them. You just sense when something is right.

The company was reborn as Set Visions Ltd but they had to think differently and devise a new business model to cut their massive overheads while still providing a highly creative imagery service. They did it using the power of computer-generated images. They are phenomenal photographers so built one kitchen, photographed it and then Chris used computer generated image (CGI) technology to change the colour, accessories and even the floor on the photos to get 25 different kitchens out of just one image.

How we sold the new technology to the clients was to place several photos side-by-side in front of the buyers and ask them to choose which was the original kitchen and which had been mainly computer-generated. They couldn't tell. It put Set Visions ahead of the curve and their customers were delighted.

It was a game-changer that saved so much money and time, not to mention the environment by preventing the need to have loads of kitchens transported to a warehouse. I invested in them for many years and they eventually bought me out in 2021. A lovely thank you.

Set Visions is now one of the largest independent CGI production companies in the UK with offices in Leeds, Sheffield and London and proudly states: "Our unique process enables us to create the very best alternative to traditional photography anywhere in the market place."

What a great success story – the phoenix out of the flames.

Another great success story is Approved Food and two guys doing amazing things to help others while continuing to grow their business.

It was about 2012 when I first met Dan Cluderay, the founder of Approved Food, and director and investor Andy Needham. Dan had been a market trader turned tech whiz kid genius who had started the business in his home while Andy was a successful wholesaler and distributor and they moved into premises in Sheffield.

Their business model was fantastic. They bought products nearing their 'best before' dates such as food, pet, household, baby food, toiletries, gifts and alcohol – to name but a few – and sold them online direct to people at around 70% cheaper than they'd pay in supermarkets.

After all, in the UK more than 7 million tonnes of food and drink is thrown away every year, a lot past its 'best before' date but still perfectly good to eat. Approved Food specialises in surplus and short-dated stock either near or just past its 'best before' date but never sell anything past its 'use by' date.

There is a big difference. 'Best before' dates give you an idea how long foods will last before they lose their quality and most last beyond this date if stored properly. Foods with a 'use by' date should be consumed before or on that date or they could start to go off.

I spent several years working with them and had I not been so busy I'd have loved to have invested and worked alongside such enterprising entrepreneurs.

They expanded and moved into premises next door to my head office at Dodworth in Barnsley and on the same site as Galpharm International Ltd.

With their slogan Waste Less Save More, they now supply more than 2,000 products and are still expanding. They went on *Dragons' Den* in 2015 asking for £150,000 in return for 10% equity but were turned down as the dragons didn't think the business was established enough and suggested profit margins were too low.

Big mistake by the dragons, as the same year Approved Food hit £4m turnover with more than 3,000 orders every week. The business continues to grow in sales, market share and profits and is a great business model.

What a company, saving people huge amounts of money on their weekly shop and delivering it to their doors while keeping thousands of products being needlessly thrown away into landfill.

Breaking into any market can be tough and the big one everyone wants is the USA, but it comes with an awful lot of hurdles and risks.

There are ways not so much round it, but ways to ease the process and we came up with one to help a brilliant Huddersfield invention that has been a godsend to people battling cancer.

Sadly, the invention came out of tragedy.

The Paxman family devised one of the first patented beer chilling processes called Brewfit. One of the founders' sons, Glenn, married Sue and they had four children, Curtis, Claire, Richard and James.

Sue was diagnosed with breast cancer in the 1990s and tried a rudimentary scalp cooling system during her chemotherapy treatment to try to stop her hair from falling out.

Unfortunately it didn't work. Sue lost her naturally curly hair and it had a devastating impact on her, especially as she was a mum with a young family and was so loved for her bright, warm and funny nature. Eventually she lost her battle with cancer in 2000, leaving her family bereft.

Glenn said: "She always put others first and was selfless. She was an amazing woman, inspirational. She was a saint."

So Glenn became determined to do all he could to prevent people going through this miserable hair loss and they used their knowledge of chilling beers to devise the Paxman Scalp Cooling System which has since been used by countless thousands of patients worldwide.

It's now very much a family-driven company with Richard the chief executive and Claire the director of global training.

By 2012 the company was very keen to move into the American market and asked me to go and see them as I may have been able to help through my knowledge of pharmaceuticals.

Glenn, Richard, Claire and Curtis are a very entrepreneurial family on a mission and such was their passion to succeed they were contemplating taking a major financial risk to get approval from the Food and Drug Administration (FDA) in the USA to get the Paxman scalp cooler into the market there.

This submission and all the red tape that involved would be very costly with no guarantee that the product would eventually be allowed into the country. The initial cost to get to this stage was estimated to be around £500,000 but, as with all these kinds of projects, there are so many unknowns. Budgets can quickly get bust and I feared it could soar towards the £1m mark.

Glenn and Richard asked if I wanted to invest in Paxman and I was deeply honoured to have been asked but declined as I felt there were too many natural entrepreneurs already involved, although I did later on.

I thought that there must be another way to get into the USA and found one to reduce both the cost and the risk.

That answer was the University of Huddersfield which looks to work with businesses in exactly this kind of scenario on what are known as Knowledge Transfer Partnerships. As an independent research establishment with considerable contacts and skills they could prepare all the technical documents, research and analysis for the FDA.

The university can access funding for doing the research and the students involved get academic recognition or even a PhD. The business ends up with evidenced-based research on the products by an independent university which can be a massive boost to a submission to the FDA.

It worked and by 2018 Paxman had gained full acceptance into the USA and continue to expand their global presence with more research and development at the University of Huddersfield in scalp cooler designs and advanced cream technology.

It was such a success that several more Knowledge Transfer Partnership projects have since been done between Paxman and the university and on such a scale that the university set up its own Paxman Scalp Cooling Research and Innovation Centre.

The real winners in all this are the people worldwide who are no longer losing their hair – along with their self-esteem and peace of mind at the toughest times in their lives – thanks to an invention inspired by a woman so deeply loved by her family and many other people.

Sue Paxman's legacy is living on as powerfully now as it did the day her family lost her.

The way business works these days is changing.

In business – especially in the 1970s and 80s – success often depended on who you knew with contacts and connections all important.

But times have changed beyond all recognition due to the internet and now it's not so much a case of who you know but how many people know you. The internet has brought direct to customer selling like never before and it's often the most effective way to operate.

The pandemic gave online shopping a massive turbo boost, so now you shop from your armchair. You need never to step outside your house again to buy anything you need – and that's everything from milk to medicines.

And with the advent of artificial intelligence it's going to go even more this way, which is rather scary so it's important everyone knows about your product and what it can do for them and all that information has to be easily found online.

Some may say it's perhaps not the most environmentally-friendly way to shop with people ordering small packets through the post but, there again, it probably saves many car journeys into towns and cities and I do think there are fewer vehicles on the roads post pandemic, especially at weekends, so maybe armchair shopping is greener after all.

But forging great working relationships is all important so if I'm travelling overseas I will often take my wife Karen and we'll go out for a meal with people from the company I'm doing business with and their wives. It forges more of a bond.

I don't like signing contracts. I prefer a handshake and if there's a problem I'll phone them or they can always phone me. Business culture is all about trust and integrity, be fair and understanding and walk a mile in other people's shoes.

A lot of the trading I do has been purely opportunistic and I still do that today.

Graham's father, Hugh, during his time in the Royal Artillery in World War Two.

Graham Leslie as a baby with mum Anne, dad Hugh and sister Annette.

Graham's love of cars can be traced back to his father, Hugh, pictured here with him as a baby.

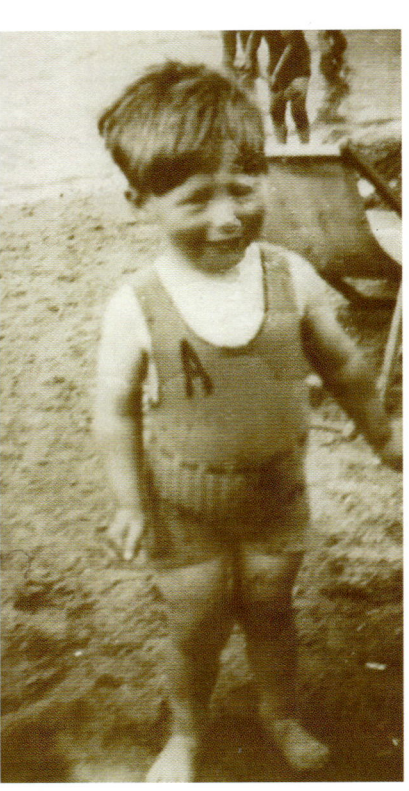

Graham on the beach in the late 1940s in his sister Annette's hand-me-down knitted swimming costume.

Graham with his mum Anne and sister Annette.

Graham's parents Hugh and Anne.

Graham and Annette Leslie with their baby brother Hugh.

Whinney Banks School where Graham was educated from 1951 to 1962.

Graham (back, third right) in his school football team at Whinney Banks.

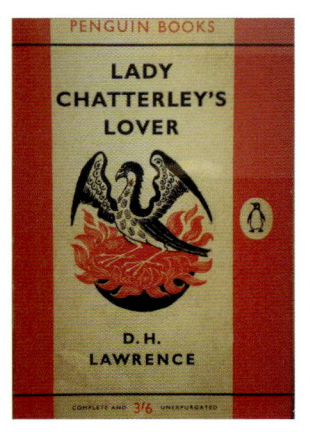

Lady Chatterley's Lover which set Graham on his entrepreneurial ways at school.

Graham (back, third right) during his footballing days with Holmbridge FC in the 1976/77 season.

Graham presenting trophies to the 2nd Battalion Boys' Brigade in Huddersfield in memory of his late father, Hugh. (Photo courtesy of *The Huddersfield Daily Examiner*)

Last Huddersfield Town match at Leeds Road April 30, 1994, with the new stadium well underway for Town's first game there on August 20, 1994, when 13,334 people saw them lose 1-0 to Wycombe Wanderers. Neil Warnock's side went on to win promotion through the play-offs into the old Division One that season. (Photo courtesy of Kirklees Stadium Development Ltd.)

Inside the John Smith's Stadium, 2024.

The Galpharm Stadium from the air showing just how much its dramatic blue stands out in the Huddersfield landscape. (Photo courtesy of *The Huddersfield Daily Examiner*)

Graham (left) and Huddersfield Town captain Peter Jackson (right) before a charity match at the old Leeds Road ground in 1994 – the last game ever played there. (Photo courtesy of *The Huddersfield Daily Examiner*)

Graham at the old Leeds Road football ground in the early 1990s. (Photo courtesy of *The Huddersfield Daily Examiner*)

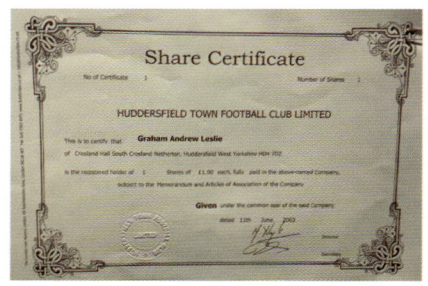

Graham's certificate as sole shareholder of just one £1 share at Huddersfield Town Football Club Limited.

Graham at the John Smith's Stadium after having his Covid jab.

The old Galpharm offices and warehouse on Foundry Street in Brighouse.

Alex and Fay Leslie at the site of the Galpharm head office in Dodworth, Barnsley, before it was built.

Galpharm head office at Dodworth near Barnsley.

Graham with former American president Bill Clinton. (Photo courtesy of *The Yorkshire Post*)

Graham with chat show legend Michael Parkinson at a charity fundraiser in Huddersfield around 2008.

Graham with Mirfield-born Hollywood star Patrick Stewart who became Chancellor at the University of Huddersfield.

Graham and his son Craig with rock legend Alice Cooper.

Graham (right) with Sarah Duchess of York and Woodman Inn cellarman David Woodhead in around 2013.

Graham's racing Ferrari that was once owned by Roger Daltrey from The Who.

Graham driving the Formula 1 car which won the Brazilian Grand Prix in 1989.

Graham at Joys Bar in Puerto Banús on the Costa del Sol in southeast Spain. Graham occasionally sang there in the 1980s and was always last on as he could empty a restaurant in two minutes.

Graham and Karen Leslie in Spain.

Graham and Karen Leslie's children and grandchildren in 2016 ...
and they now have 6 more grandchildren.

Graham in his University of Huddersfield gown when he received his Honorary Doctorate in Business and Administration. (Photo courtesy of The University of Huddersfield)

Graham presented with his CBE by Prince William.

Graham receives his CBE at Buckingham Palace with sister Annette and brother Hugh.

Graham and composer Benson Taylor (left) with The Kingdom Choir leader Karen Gibson and its music arranger and producer Jonathan Owusu-Yianomah outside Abbey Road Studios in London in December 2023.

Graham playing guitar with his granddaughter Matilda Briddon.

Graham playing guitar outside the Woodman Inn at Thunderbridge.

Artist Richard Gower's painting of the Duke of Edinburgh on his final Royal engagement which he gave to The Queen.

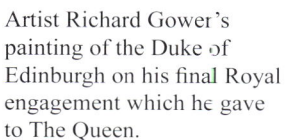

Graham and artist Richard Gower with Richard's painting of Christopher Schindler scoring the penalty that put Huddersfield Town into the Premier League in 2017.

Kindest Regards

Professor Graham A. Leslie, C.B.E.   Hon. D.B.A
Apprentice Chairman

Richard Gower's watercolour of The Kingdom Choir on Graham's music for his song 'United Together'.

One of Graham's promo pictures.

Graham's crest, designed by his brother, Hugh, depicting the stadium and ibuprofen molecules while the belt is part of the Leslie clan crest from his Scottish heritage.

People who attend Waves day care centre in Slaithwaite. All proceeds from this autobiography are going to the centre's charity, Making Waves.

The Leslie Business Barometer ... how to keep moving forward in business

The barometer is a basic for business, but so important.

Get a sheet of paper and write five headings on it – sales, stock, debtors, creditors and cash – with columns below you can fill in each week.

Then write in the figures for each one every Friday afternoon. You'll soon see if you've too much stock or are chasing debtors and it works exactly the same no matter the size of your business from a single seat hairdressing salon to a multi-national corporation.

In the same vein you need a five-year rolling business plan with each year split into four quarters. Start with the plan for the first quarter for the first year and then fill in what you hope to have achieved by the fourth quarter in the fifth year.

Then go back and fill in the steps you think you'll need to take every quarter to achieve your ultimate ambition and check at the end of each quarter if you've made them. If you haven't, figure how much you're off course and then work out a plan to get it back on track. Business success is all about constantly checking and reworking.

But also know what your competitors are doing too so research them. At Galpharm we had a monthly meeting dedicated to finding out what our rivals were up to from what they were selling to how their warehouse and logistics operated. You need that in every business. Learn what your competitors are doing and then work out a way to do it better. Most businesses never think to do this at all.

At Galpharm we would always be questioning, asking our warehouse staff about carton costs, the latest racking systems, the best forklift trucks. Accounts would be asked to look into the latest legislation on the horizon and find out who gave the best exchange rates, especially as we were importing 90% of store brand pharmaceuticals from factories in India at the time.

Every department should always be questioning and never be content to just stand still as that ultimately leads to stagnation. We'd have these planning meetings every Monday morning from 8am to 10pm so they could be put into action during the week.

In business you always need an open mind and be prepared to learn.

That's not to say you always get it right. We did really well in the mid-1980s selling lip balms and our first massive order was through Superdrug so we got all excited and set up our own lip balm manufacturing base on our Dodworth site to make our own brand.

We expected hundreds to roll off the production line every hour but were only getting around 100. We had the machinery manufacturers back time and time again but nothing seemed to improve output.

Then, suddenly, one day we shot up to 500 tubes of lip balm an hour. We were puzzled. What could have made such a dramatic difference?

The mystery was solved when one of our production line staff happened to mention that the only other person who had been near the machinery was the cleaner and she'd started to spray polish on it and then wipe it down. For some reason, just doing that had turbo-charged the production line.

When she came in the following day I asked to see her in my office. She was worried as she feared she'd lose her job for tampering with the machinery. Instead, I thanked her, gave her a £2,000 bonus and told her to spend it on a holiday. The bonus came from the profits earned by the increasing production.

Word quickly spread and soon everyone was trying to come up with good ideas to enhance Galpharm's profits. And, yes, all the ones that worked were well rewarded which is all part of teamwork and everyone feeling valued.

The lip balm production idea was less successful. Eventually we realised that manufacturing lip balm was costing too much in terms of energy, resources and time and so outsourced it once more which ended up being a far more efficient option. We even gave the company our machinery to make it on.

It's important in business to know when something isn't working quite how it should and then take what can be tough decisions to accept it's wrong and do something about it.

In 1998 we held a very different Christmas party. The John Godber play *Bouncers* was at the Lawrence Batley Theatre in Huddersfield to mark 21 years since it had been written. I arranged a private showing for our staff and it's a Christmas party they still remember today just because it was so different. Some had never been to live theatre before and it was held in the cellar bar so they were right next to the actors, almost to the point they felt to be part of the play.

The arts is vital to a thriving community spirit so Galpharm was a founder patron of the LBT which was a fantastic community effort to get it built at a cost just over £5m. Dame Judi Dench laid the foundation stone in 1992 and it was opened by Mirfield-born Sir Patrick Stewart – who went on to become Chancellor at the University of Huddersfield between 2004 and 2015 – on September 11, 1994.

Finally there's the Leslie Beaufort Scale for business that's for three, six and nine years – like the Beaufort wind scale but for business.

The first three years are the most crucial with 70% of new businesses usually failing in this timescale.

Why? Well, it's often because they haven't researched if there's a real need for what they're offering. Is there really a demand for that product or service or can their customers get it elsewhere cheaper and better? You need to supply the market with what it wants and the trick and skill is knowing what it wants.

I've been there, creating a warm toilet seat by hooking it up to the central heating system. Trouble was, no-one wanted it.

Many people set off in a new business with passion, enthusiasm and a blind belief they can make it work, no matter what, but they often have very limited experience running a business and all the costs and potential pitfalls that entails.

Entrepreneurs need a good 'diet' so if they have too many products in the warehouse they turn to fat. To use another analogy, you wouldn't fill your car with petrol if all you were going to do was park it on the driveway.

Anyone who runs a successful business needs a business brain and that's all about input and output. If you're putting more in than you're getting out then it's not going to work.

Or, as Charles Dickens's wonderful character Wilkins Micawber warned in his classic novel *David Copperfield*: "Annual income twenty pounds, annual expenditure nineteen pounds, nineteen and six. Result happiness. Annual income twenty pounds, annual expenditure twenty pounds and six. Result misery."

He was certainly right. You have to make a profit in business or you won't have one for long. For Mr Micawber the result was more dire – the gates of a debtors' prison closing behind him.

So, the first three years are very risky but once you get over them and reach six years you've a good chance of surviving. By nine years your business should be safe with secure foundations and that gale of the first three years should have toned down to a light breeze.

It's also important to get the right people and for them to stay loyal to the company … and that's a two-way stretch.

I usually have the sense if a person is right within the first 30 seconds of meeting them – that first contact and handshake is all important – but if it's a job interview don't forget it's a two-way thing too. If there is an applicant you really want don't forget you have to 'sell' the company to them too to make them want to join and stay. It's not all about the business doing the hiring.

You often find that people fit into what's known as 'the plumber's theory' – are they a drain or a radiator. Drains are pessimistic and, actually, sap your strength and patience while radiators radiate optimism and help to invigorate both you and your business.

I once went for an interview in the 1970s for a sales job at Cadbury Schweppes but the interview was all one way. They told me what the salary was during the interview which was less than I was on at the time. I pointed this out and asked why they thought I'd leave my current job for a role with them. The answer was: "Well, we're Cadbury Schweppes."

There was an arrogance about the whole interview that left me cold so I walked out of the building deciding I definitely didn't want to join them.

You also have to think on your feet so much in business.

During the Galpharm years we did a lot of business with a great company in Wexford on the southwest coast of Ireland called Medentech which produced sterilising tablets for baby bottles and utensils.

They also did water purification tablets for the World Health Organization so I bought shares in them. I thought I could get Medentech a lot of business with Superdrug so arranged for representatives from Superdrug to visit the factory.

I was on my way to the factory with the visitors when they rang me to say they'd had a flood and could I delay them so we diverted to the nearest restaurant for an early lunch. We parked up and went to the door to find it locked and a sign hanging there which said 'Gone For Lunch'. How ironic.

Time for Plan B, which was a charming country pub with a waterwheel. I rushed into the bar, ordered some drinks and asked the landlord: "What time do you close?"

"October," he replied.

And, after all that, the flood was quickly sorted and we landed the contract.

You also need to be aware and savvy in business and in the early days at Galpharm one of the most crucial tools of the trade was a Stanley knife and a steady hand. Our traded products came from suppliers in cardboard boxes with their name and sometimes address stamped onto the box itself.

As we were usually shipping these boxes straight out to customers we had to carefully slice the top layer of carboard off to remove the other company's details. We didn't want our customers going straight to our suppliers and cutting out the middleman which, at that time, was Galpharm. Slicing that cardboard to remove the name without leaving a mark became quite a surgical skill.

Luck and persistence are also two things you need in business and the example that springs to mind involves chemist Dr Spencer Silver. Now the name – which is a wonderful name – may not be instantly recognisable but you'll know the product he invented. It was the Post-it note.

Spencer worked for multinational American company 3M and was experimenting trying to find a super tough glue but accidentally came up with an adhesive that stuck lightly to surfaces but didn't bond to them – exactly the opposite of what he was trying to do.

He thought there must be a use for them, but didn't quite know what, yet kept going on about it to colleagues to the point he became known as Mr Persistent.

Another scientist who worked with him at 3M, Art Fry – another brilliant name – was in a church choir and used to pop little scraps of paper in the pages to mark the hymns they were going to sing but, inevitably, the paper kept falling out leaving him, well, frustrated.

He then had a hallelujah moment – well, he was in a church choir – by recalling Spencer's adhesive and the two of them got together to invent the Post-it note.

The rest, as they say, is history, and Spencer once put it wonderfully, saying that like many ground-breaking innovations theirs was a product nobody thought they needed until they did.

And that's the perfect business invention.

My businesses close to home

I'm sometimes asked if there's much of a difference between how family businesses and corporate ones operate.

You bet there is. There's a huge gulf and it returns to my analogy of a tanker and a speedboat. You don't need to be a Hercule Poirot or Miss Marple to work out which is which.

Corporates are often bogged down by so much structure, procedure and routine which often attracts the kind of staff who like that rigidity.

Family-run businesses tend to be smaller with a workforce that needs to be more dynamic and creative with flexible people who can adapt their skills to changing needs. Galpharm always had that family-run ethos. We wanted our staff to think differently, to challenge us with new ideas to produce new products and explore new markets.

It's easy for businesses to come up with catchy slogans, usually promising to put the customer first, but how many corporates actually do? They are so big they don't have to really 'buy into it' and where does the responsibility for that start and end? This mission statement culture is easy enough to write but implementing it properly is what ultimately counts.

In a family business people tend to fully understand the real concept and importance of customers. Without them you don't have a business. It's as stark and simple as that. Everyone gained is an increase in profits and everyone lost a decrease.

That's why I started Galpharm in the first place, as the corporate culture I worked in just wouldn't accept my new, creative ideas, so I went off to work with someone who would … myself.

Power and paranoia can run rife in the corporate world but if it rears its head in the family-run one it needs to be quickly managed and controlled.

Family businesses know the value of every employee and how hard it can be to replace the really good ones. At Galpharm we never had an HR department. My door was always open, so anyone who worked for Galpharm could come to see me straightaway.

We didn't even have a marketing department. The sales team on the ground knew what sold, what didn't and what the customers wanted. That was all rounded up in a weekly meeting.

Everyone in the company had an incentive to help drive Galpharm forward. If someone came up with an idea that we then developed into a product, the employee received the first month's profits from that product's sales.

Likewise, if they spotted a way to make Galpharm more cost-effective, then they'd get the first three months of the savings as a bonus.

Everyone benefits from this culture which is totally inclusive. Anyone could come up with an idea which means everyone was committed to working to the same end, namely for the good of the company.

And that's why family businesses are often so strong with loyal staff and an ethos that we are all in it together.

And that was behind another commercial venture.

One of the first pubs I went in when I arrived in Huddersfield in 1971 was The Woodman Inn at Thunderbridge. It's a real country pub set in a wooded vale and well-known throughout Huddersfield. I went on to buy it with my son, Craig, just over 40 years later.

My affection for the place grew after I met my second wife, Ann, there in around 1977, having seen her as a shop assistant at Boots chemists in the nearby village of Kirkburton, and we went on to have two gorgeous children, son Alex in 1986 and daughter Fay in 1988.

Ann was very attractive and loved swimming, but I was 32 and separated with two children which certainly shocked and disappointed her mother. We were together for five years before marrying in 1982 and were then together for 10 years and have always remained friendly.

Ann was an original shareholder in Galpharm, a great supporter of me setting up in business, a loving mum to our two children and an exceptionally talented photographer.

A further connection came as my head of planning in the stadium company Kirklees Stadium Developments Ltd, Paul Sykes, lived across the road from The Woodman, so in 2000 I asked him to let me know if he ever heard rumours the pub was up for sale. The call came in 2012 and by June that year the pub was ours.

My original plan was to buy the pub as an investment through my pension fund and then rent it out to a tenant to provide a steady income. But my son Craig had other ideas and persuaded me The Woodman had fantastic potential. It had several bedrooms but the occupancy rate was only around 10%.

He was right. It just needed vision, the right people to run it day-by-day, plus lots of drive and determination.

First the people. David Woodhead had been one of Huddersfield's most respected landlords and beer experts for decades and wherever he was his loyal clientele followed. We also took on a very experienced local chef and then brought in a two-star Michelin chef from the highly respected Box Tree restaurant in Ilkley.

My wife, Karen, created the designs and relaxing country ambience for the inn and bedrooms and we eventually bought Paul's house across the road and transformed that into six more bedrooms and a downstairs unique chef's experience. In short, the chef was at work and customers could sit in there to watch, learn and help him.

The aim then was to turn The Woodman into Yorkshire's premier wedding venue. In the end we had 20 bedrooms and transformed a neighbouring cottage owned by Karen into a three-bedroomed bridal preparation suite. The venue was booked just about every week for sometimes two or three weddings and became phenomenally successful. Everything was geared to that big day. No detail could ever be too small.

When The Woodman wasn't being used for a wedding it was ideal for business events and conferences, especially for overseas guests being hosted by Huddersfield companies as it was the quintessential English country inn. So much better and memorable than a 'bedroom factory' next to a motorway.

It also had its characters. The Woodman is set in a hollow with the road leading down to it in both directions. One local always sat in a corner with his own tankard and if a stranger came in he'd say to them: "Does tha' fancy a bet? Tha's come down the road to get here and the only way out is to go up. I'll bet thee a fiver I can leave here and walk downhill."

If anyone took up the bet he'd stand up, walk out of the pub, cross the road, walk into the stream opposite and then wade downstream.

He'd then amble back in with his legs soaked to pick up his winnings.

So, with The Woodman I'd lost a local and gained a great business, but venues like this are intense places to run so after 10 years we decided that was it and sold it to Lancashire-based Robinsons Brewery which was expanding into Yorkshire and now has 25 pubs.

We'd achieved what we could with The Woodman and knew it was time to move on, knowing it was in safe hands for the future.

We'd kept its tradition, warmth and heritage but turned it into something special.

The Woodman, though, had also taught me the importance of data to back up gut feelings or even replace them.

I discovered through the University of Huddersfield that data can be vital when plotting a business. Gut feeling plays a part but it's best to be backed up by some facts and solid statistics. The university's Head of Corporate Policy, James Devitt, is an expert on collecting data and, although I knew The Woodman's location was paramount to its success, I didn't know why so to progress my business model I needed to understand the demographics of why this location worked so well.

I asked James to look at it for me and examined the population demographics at three, five and 10 miles out from the Woodman. The demographics include age profiles, property values, people's earnings, the number of schools, care homes and lots more information that would indicate why a pub like The Woodman would work well where it did.

The information helped shape the price point for the menus and bedrooms and also revealed there was very little competition around in this upmarket pub market so massively helped with marketing too.

From that depth of information it's possible to plan and develop a complete business model which my son Craig and his wife, Sarah, implemented and one that proved to be very successful.

I asked James if he could find me another nine of these locations in the north of England where we could replicate what we'd done at The Woodman and would be an attractive proposition for investors.

We had proved the concept, delivered the model and so would be a pretty safe bet for investors. That, of course, is in a pre-Covid world. In the end, we decided not to take the plan for 10 'Woodmans' around the north of England forward as we ended up too busy with other projects.

James did the same when we were thinking of opening some shops in the UK for a baby products company we had set up called Babyway. His data showed where the high birth areas would be in the country over the next 10 years and so would be the best spots for the shops.

There's an awful lot of science in data and without it you could be basing your business on not much more than a hunch and guesswork. Data may well throw up something you didn't know about or expect and lead to a radical rethink. But, there again, it may just prove your gut feeling was correct all along.

If you want to know why China is often ahead of the game when it comes to manufacturing, here's perhaps why.

Babyway was run by my second son, Alex, and my daughter Fay. Many of the baby nursery products were sourced from China, so in 2010 I took Alex out there and what we saw opened our eyes like never before. We landed in Hong Kong and then took a bullet train to Guangzhou, a sprawling port city northwest of Hong Kong on the Pearl River.

Once we arrived we were driven on a five-lane highway with no cars on it passing empty warehouses and offices on a vacant industrial estate and there was even a sports stadium there. Eerily, all were empty.

I was told it was all ready for China's looming industrial revolution which was set to take off at the time.

They did a trade show in Guangzhou which must be the world's biggest as you can buy anything from a paper clip to a car there. I ended up bartering with a bloke about a Tempa Dot disposable baby thermometer when we got stuck on the price. He insisted on $1.50 but I said that's all I could sell them for each in the UK so there would be no profit for me.

He stared at me in disbelief, shook his head and proclaimed: "You're stupid. The $1.50 price is for a dozen."

Well, that certainly rapidly changed the deal's complexion. You should never think you know it all.

The business grew quickly but then some of the businesses we sold the products through started to demand they did their own checks on our Chinese and Thailand manufacturers even though they already surpassed British standards. What's more, our distributors demanded we pay the whole bill for them, including first-class travel, so when that starts to happen it's time to shut up shop and move on, which we did. It was fortunate too as the market then nosedived with such huge names as Mothercare and Mamas and Papas being badly hit with the entire sector in decline.

Some time ago my company GL Properties built 44 homes on seven sites in the Castleford and Pontefract areas, which are all rented out to make sure people have quality properties and a few are bungalows for the elderly.

They are now all professionally managed on my behalf by Nicola Hale, a fantastic example of someone brilliant at multi-skilling who organises everything from lettings, finances and maintenance to sorting out all legal legislation. She manages it incredibly smoothly and is so loyal to the Leslie cause of helping others whenever she can.

In the early days of Galpharm one of the north's best-known cash and carry warehouses was a massive support to me.

It was Nield Cash and Carry based in the infamously tough area of Cheetham Hill next to Strangeways Prison in Manchester run by an amazing entrepreneur, Ted Clague. He'd helped me to shift surplus Winthrop Pharmaceutical stocks in the 1970s so when I started Galpharm in the early 1980s I went to see Ted and asked his advice on how to get my fledgling business up and running.

He must have seen something in me because he said straightaway I'd go on to make a fortune. It really boosted my confidence at a time when I was divorced with no money, was living in rented accommodation and had borrowed £5,000 from the bank to get started.

The advice he gave was profound and has stayed with me forever. It was about business relationships and trust.

He said always allow the next person to make a profit – that way they will always come back to do business with you. It's fine to negotiate hard but always be fair. That's the civilised way to create successful commercial relationships and be successful in business.

Ted's advice then went one better after I'd been going for around a year. He told me to set up my own personal pension scheme which was absolutely the last thing on my mind but it was the best advice anyone ever gave me.

I did set one up and the way the regulations were with this pre-1989 scheme I could use it like my own personal bank to buy property and then rent it out with the rent flowing back into the pension scheme. It was the way I ended up funding Galpharm without any risk from banks foreclosing and it saved me an awful lot of money along the way in bank interest charges too. We've been through recessions in 1990 and 2008 and how many businesses have ended up being shut down by the banks in those?

Ted was so kind-hearted he gave me an old pallet truck in the very early days even though Galpharm didn't have a warehouse and placed weekly and monthly orders to help me get the business off the ground. I delivered them to him in my white Transit van. After all, Galpharm only had one employee back then but he was certainly committed to the cause. That sole employee was me.

Over the next 25 years Nield's grew into a huge trading and distribution wholesaler and cash and carry business with annual sales over £80m by the millennium and Galpharm hadn't done bad either.

Things began to slide for Nield's as they became less competitive in an increasingly tough market and in 2015 one of Ted's sons said they were looking to sell the business and would we be interested?

My son, Craig, was looking for a new challenge so we bought Nield's and transformed it from a traditional cash and carry to a bulk distribution trading company that bought truckloads of quality products made by the likes of Gillette and Procter and Gamble and sold them by the pallet load to wholesalers, corner shop chains and cash and carry outlets while also massively increasing exports.

We ended up being a very successful middleman and that was down to strength of contacts. Its turnover doubled each year for the first three years to become one of the fastest growing export companies in the UK.

How the University of Huddersfield ended up with its first non-academic Resident Professor of Enterprise and Entrepreneurship

I met my third wife Karen in the car park at the large Sainsbury's store on Huddersfield ring road.

I was stocking up for my daughter ahead of a business trip to India and she was shopping with her daughter after returning from Spain, ironically having stayed just around the corner from my villa there.

We chatted briefly but the attraction was immediate. We met again at Da Sandro Italian restaurant at Birchencliffe the lunchtime I landed bank from India and the rest is history. To think I nearly went to Aldi!

The year was 2005 and Karen worked at the University of Huddersfield as head of the department for international students in places such as Hong Kong and Kuala Lumpur studying transport and logistics courses through a distance learning degree course.

People at the university began to wonder who I was, especially as I was always picking her up from work and my company's name, Galpharm, was by then on the stadium.

That started my long association with the university which changed my whole world and continues today. It was all due to that wonderful day when I met my gorgeous wife in Sainsbury's car park.

It shows the importance of connections as it led to everything. If that chance meeting hadn't happened I don't think I would have been recognised at the university, been involved at the 3M, received my honour as Resident Professor of Enterprise and Entrepreneurship or even, perhaps, got my CBE.

The university's Professor of Entrepreneurship asked me to give a lecture in 2006 about my journey in business and around 200 students attended, along with several people from the university and successful business leaders.

I walked in with a Vileda mop, a paper clip and a guitar. The mop grabbed their attention. After all, why would anyone walk around carrying a mop? The paper clip was a way of showing them how to open their minds and think out of the box about the many ways you could use a paper clip and the guitar was to show that most people have a hidden skill.

Even today, not a lot of people know I play music and write songs with my particular skill being able to empty a restaurant in three minutes.

The underlying theme was simple. To set off on a successful route in life you need to be motivated and inspired. That first step is the biggest one and then, after that, simply don't look back. Just keep looking forward.

It also turned out myself and the University of Huddersfield vice chancellor Professor Bob Cryan had an important business idea in common.

I told him I'd registered a company called The Yorkshire Business Academy and designed a potential building for it at Dodworth near Barnsley where Galpharm was based. The whole concept was to give fledgling businesses a vital start – a leg up, if you like. This was because statistics showed that Yorkshire had the highest rate of new start-ups in the country but around 70% failed in the first two or three years. I wanted to do something to change that.

The new small and medium enterprises would be on the ground floor and we'd help them with experienced mentors and volunteers specialising in their sector of commerce, along with the knowledge and wisdom of an accountant.

If the business was still a goer after a year they would move up to the second floor and could have a further two years there but would then have to leave and find their own premises. They had to be able to stand on their own two feet after the three years. If they couldn't by then, chances were they never would.

Bob was amazed. It was almost identical to a scheme he was setting up in a refurbished former woollen mill on Firth Street near Huddersfield town centre, so he suggested I join him in the venture and even offered me a suite in the building which became the 3M Buckley Innovation Centre.

It was perfect and I got on exceptionally well with Professor Liz Towns-Andrews, OBE, 3M Professor of Innovation at the University of Huddersfield. We were from the same culture and mindset about the need to bridge academia with the commercial world and to do this would give creative and innovative businesses the opportunity to access the knowledge and equipment at the university.

The 3M Buckley was the ideal way to do this, especially through Knowledge Transfer Partnerships (KTP) that would give companies access to university staff, students, equipment, services and research at a fraction of the cost ... and still does.

For instance, there is measuring equipment at the university that is worth hundreds of thousands of pounds as it goes down to the finest possible margins – the kind of equipment no start-up could ever hope to afford in its early years. It's the same for research labs, engineering and energy companies, tech development and 3D printing.

Also, if they turned to a private company to do this for them it would cost them the full price, whereas at the university the cost would be more likely split 50/50 while also giving students the chance to do in-depth research in 'real world' scenarios with the business, leading to higher qualifications such as Masters and PhDs. It's also a way the students can find jobs in the high tech, creative industries.

Many students who join businesses on Knowledge Transfer Partnerships are so impressive they end up staying there once they've finished their studies. The more universities link in with local, national and even international businesses, the better the job prospects for their students.

I still firmly believe the student loan system is immoral. No-one should have to pay for a university education and then leave there with a degree but heavily in debt for a long period of their lives.

Graduates need to be ready for that world of work but it's not always the case. Some university courses simply won't lead straight to jobs without further qualifications once the student has graduated.

Huddersfield University leads the way in focusing on life after university and you can't see it in a more highly visual way than its new landmark £250m National Health Innovation Campus which drives forward excellence in healthcare training from specialist clinical teaching to dental hygiene. There is also a Health and Wellbeing Innovation Centre for local entrepreneurs or start-ups and organisations looking to benefit from locating onto the campus.

The health campus will also have a Community Diagnostic Centre (CDC) Hub developed in partnership with Calderdale and Huddersfield NHS Foundation Trust and the first of its kind at a university.

The CDC will provide access to thousands of diagnostic tests for the people of Huddersfield and Calderdale, including MRI and CT scanners.

My role at the 3M Buckley was voluntary, holding surgeries and advising the new start-ups at an early stage and then seeing how they were progressing as time moved on. These have included engineering, pharmaceuticals, IT, transport and logistics. Then there are companies that measure vibration of component parts which is absolutely critical to industry. They'll investigate vibrations in aircraft engines and on submarines where 100% accuracy is critical. When you're 35,000ft in the air or dozens of metres below the surface of the sea the last thing you want is a vital nut or screw working itself loose.

Some of the work that goes on at the university is highly commercially sensitive and these projects can change and preserve lives.

After a couple of years these fledgling businesses should have grown enough to leave the 3M and move into their own premises and, if they remain in the Huddersfield area, so much the better for the local economy and jobs.

The University of Huddersfield buildings now dominate the skyline and that's a physical manifestation of how important it is to the town, from attracting more than 20,000 students to helping them to get the skills and experience to set up their own creative businesses here once they've graduated or find work with our local companies.

I ended up becoming a non-academic academic, if you see what I mean. First I was awarded an honorary doctorate in 2006, then six years later made a Visiting Professor of Enterprise and Entrepreneurship and I'm now Resident Professor of Enterprise and Entrepreneurship, the first non-academic person to hold such a role in the university's history.

After 10 years I gave up my suite to allow more room for new start-up businesses and remain a committed board member at the 3M Buckley.

Not bad for a lad from the North East who left school with dyslexia and no recognised qualifications.

You can't beat the qualifications of life's experiences. They are the lessons you'll never forget.

The strange way I met Bill Clinton ... and some other great Graham tales

You never know what's going to happen over the next 24 hours.

I've a cracking story which sums this up perfectly.

My sister, Annette, called me from Canada to say her daughter, Victoria, who was working at the University of Oxford had been chosen to welcome former US President Bill Clinton's daughter, Chelsea, who was about to do a PhD there ... but swore me to secrecy and not tell a soul.

I was then due to attend a business conference attended by 2,000 people in a giant marquee in York and who should be the main guest speaker but Bill Clinton.

That man has a charisma all his own. The top business people throughout Yorkshire were there but his presence is unbelievable and he received a standing ovation both before and after his speech.

I was sitting next to someone very high up in Australia Bank and he said he could get me to meet Bill Clinton backstage. I jumped at the chance, went through the extra security and found myself at the back on a long queue of dignitaries to meet the ex-president.

Everyone was lined up looking at the main door expectantly, but the next thing I felt a tap on my shoulder and turned round to find Bill Clinton standing next to me. He'd come in the wrong door.

I shook his hand, told him his speech was great and, by the way, Chelsea was in good hands with my niece, Victoria. I think the fact I was telling Bill Clinton this allowed me to break my sister's confidence.

He asked how I knew that and I replied: "Victoria's my niece."

He did his meet-and-greet, but before he left said, "I just need a quick word with Graham."

He came back over and asked what I was doing the next night.

I replied: "Whatever I'm doing I can change."

But he thanked me for introducing me to everyone and walked off so I never knew what he had in mind.

It just shows you never know what's going to happen in your life from one minute to the next so make sure every 24 hours counts and wake up every day happy to be alive.

You'll be amazed where life can suddenly take you next.

In the early 1990s Galpharm was trading internationally with branded products like Gillette G11 blades, Wilkinson Sword blades, BIC disposable razors and Colgate toothpaste with most of our supply negotiations done in and around Marbella and Puerto Banus, so if I booked a three-day trip it would inevitably turn into five.

We'd often do the negotiations in the Red Pepper restaurant in Puerto Banus, then a drink next door at the world-famous Sinatra Bar.

One night Craig and I decided to have a cheeky one at this famous haunt of the wealthy and famous on the way back to our hotel.

While we were sitting at the bar a lady tapped me on the shoulder and said, "Would you like a dance?"

"Love to," I replied and off we went.

After 15 or so minutes dancing – sometimes quite close – I returned the lady to her VIP table and guests. I recognised one as Peter Reid so, never wanting to miss an opportunity and having recently become a director of Huddersfield Town, I introduced myself to Peter.

I even suggested he might consider becoming Town's new player coach, gave him my business card and returned to Craig who was still sitting at the bar.

"Do you know who that was?" asked Craig.

"Yes," I said. "Peter Reid and I've asked if he wants to become involved with Town."

Craig looked at me perplexed.

"No, the lady you've just been dancing with."

"No," I said. "I've no idea, although I wondered if she was an escort or someone like that."

Craig finished his drink and said: "Come on, Dad, it's time to go. If you can't recognise actress Cindy Crawford when you've danced with her there's no hope for you."

As we left I gazed across and there she was sat with Richard Gere.

The Red Pepper restaurant was owned by an ex Greek navy captain, an amazing character who sat there every night supervising his staff and on one occasion we were in there and the kitchen caught fire so we all had to evacuate the building quickly.

Next morning I went back to pay our bill and ended up helping him to clear up. The owner said we were the only people from the previous night to come back, check how they all were and pay their bill.

From then on we had the best table in the house whenever we went – the one Lady Di sat at when she once ate there – and the owner always sent over an appetiser.

So never forget. Treat people how you would like to be treated.

The Marbella area is one where you are likely to bump into celebrities ranging from the notorious to the legendary.

In the late 1990s I was at the Don Leoni restaurant in Puerto Banus when I met Monica Lewinsky, famous for that supposed 'dalliance' with Bill Clinton.

Another time in the same restaurant I found myself sitting next to the original James Bond, Sean Connery, and his wife as they lived near Marbella and we had a chat about Scotland and my Highland dancing.

If you can be 'flexible' with the truth it can potentially land you in the mire.

Karen and I were on holiday in Monaco and had always wanted to go to the magnificent five-star Hotel De Paris in Monte Carlo.

As soon as we walked in we realised we were very underdressed to go to its café, but thought we'd give it a go and asked at reception if we could pop in for a drink and some cake.

The receptionist took one look at us and said: "The tables are all full, I'm sorry."

I wasn't giving up that easily and so thought who was famous and is linked to Monaco and the only person that immediately came to mind was easyJet founder Sir Stelios Haji-Ioannou, so I said we were there for a meeting with him.

The man at reception then said: "No problem. Follow me."

He led us into the café and within minutes a bottle of champagne and two glasses arrived. I began to worry as I only had so much cash on me and wasn't sure the limit on my debit card would cover it.

There were two English couples on the next table and the maître d then arrived and said our friend was here.

In walked Stelios and headed in our direction. Just as I thought the game was up he sat down with the two English couples – he must have been meeting them. After a short while they all got up and walked out.

The maître d returned and said: "Hurry up, your friend is leaving without you. Here's the bill."

Needless to say, after paying it we had no money for a taxi … and not much else either.

The moral is, be careful how you bluff your way into something as you may not get out of it so easily.

Ironically, I had in mind an idea for kennels and catteries near all major airports as people love their pets so much they could drop them off last minute and then pick them up shortly after they land back. I'd have called it easyPet.

The naivety of some people can be astounding, but also highly entertaining.

We were on holiday in Florida at a bar where there was a somewhat brash American bragging about what his grandad and dad had done and it was getting to such a stage I felt a reality check was needed.

So I said: "It's interesting what you're saying as we've had some great success in our family too. In fact, my great great great grandfather invented and patented the full stop."

It stopped the American in his tracks. He looked straight at me in amazement and said: "Really? Is that how you made your money?"

I replied: "Yes, absolutely. Every time someone uses a full stop we get a royalty for it. But it led to a family fallout as his brother then invented the comma and my great great great grandfather insisted he'd stolen the idea from him."

"Wow," said the American. "That's unbelievable, man."

Yet he believed it even though I'd made it all up. I just loved the wonderful naivety.

We have a villa in Sotogrande in Spain and many years ago Sarah, Duchess of York was there presenting trophies at a world series polo competition.

She was on her own behind a little red rope to keep the supporters away so I grabbed a couple of polo balls, went round the back of the stage, walked up behind her and said: "Excuse me, ma'am, but could you sign my balls, please?"

She turned round, somewhat shocked but laughed when she saw the polo balls and I explained they would be auctioned off to raise money for testicular cancer. She duly signed them and we became close friends years later when we met again when she visited the University of Huddersfield. One of her daughters, Princess Beatrice, later became patron at the Forget Me Not Children's Hospice.

I'd always dreamed of owning my own boat ever since passing my off-shore sailing certificate at Largs in Scotland in the 1970s ... but it was pure fantasy at that point.

So when, in 2004, I was able to afford one I bought a 40ft cruiser, took her out to Sotogrande Marina in Spain and named her *Fantasea*.

Although I'd started to see Karen in 2005 I was still single and so texted ladies I knew and asked if any wanted to go on a cruising course on the boat ... and they'd also have to go on a submarine in

Murmansk. I wanted to see just how keen they were. The submarine was no more than a red herring.

Only Karen replied to say: "I'm with you."

So we boarded the plane to Gibraltar and, while reading up on the cruising manual, Karen asked if the 'sharp end of the boat' was the bow or the stern.

I thought, "This is going to be a long week," but she certainly proved me wrong as just four days later our sailing tutor asked Karen to negotiate a route back from Gibraltar to Sotogrande in our cruiser at night and in fog.

She passed the test ... but I had to go back the next day to complete mine!

So *Fantasea* became our boat and my sailing prowess became so bad at one stage I was known as The Crasher of Sotogrande Marina when trying to berth.

We sold *Fantasea* years ago and I know we both miss the freedom and pleasure she gave us.

I've a friend involved in a distillery in Scotland and about 20 years ago they had a single malt whisky that had been left to mature for 20 years, but for the final few weeks they'd put it in some red wine barrels to add a hint of a fruit flavour.

When they drew the whisky off at the Bruichladdich distillery on the Isle of Islay they discovered that the barrel's effect was far more than fruity as it had turned the whisky pink.

They asked me for advice on what to do with the 5,000 bottles and I suggested market it as a special edition for women and export it to China and Japan where they'd pay well for such a one-off whisky. To enhance the marketing even more they called it Flirtation.

They sent me a case by way of thanks and I still have a couple of bottles. They'll be 40 years old now.

At the end of the 1990s I bought the magnificent Crosland Hall set in the countryside near Meltham.

We were doing the library up and needed some moulded plaster coving. The builder had been involved in restoration work on Windsor Castle after its devastating fire in November 1992 and had some coving left over so we decided to use that.

We knew it was destined for Windsor Castle as it has ER etched on it but the Queen never knew our library had the royal seal of approval.

Talking of royalty I have a confession to make ... as a teenager I had a crush on Princess Anne, the Princess Royal.

It began when I was around 15 or 16 in 1961 and my dad had delivered a lad to Borstal near York in his role as probation officer and I was in the car.

We were ushered off to the side of the road as a convoy was coming past with the royals in it returning from a wedding nearby.

As I watched the cars go past there was a young Princess Anne and Prince Charles in an open-top Rolls Royce. Princess Anne looked at me and waved so I waved back. She was younger than me but I thought she looked lovely with her blonde, curly hair.

Many years later she became Patron of the Carers Trust charity. I, along with the charity's supporters nationwide, performed my Christmas song on Spotify and YouTube to raise money for the trust in around 2018, so me and Karen were invited to the charity's Christmas carol service in London and then to a dinner. I was gobsmacked when I looked at the place settings and discovered I was sitting next to Princess Anne.

Karen said to her: "I'll apologise for him now."

Princess Anne replied: "Why, does he come with a Government health warning?"

Karen was amazed as that's exactly what I'd said to her on our first date: "I should come with a Government health warning."

I couldn't resist telling Princess Anne about my teenage crush and she was brilliant all evening and incredibly chatty. Her commitment to her royal role is phenomenal.

I'm Lord of the Manor of Greetland and the way I ended up with the title all happened by chance, especially as I've never lived in Greetland.

I'd just landed a big contract for Galpharm with Superdrug in July 1986 to provide them their own brand washing machine liquid shortly after the big names, Surf and Persil, had launched their own brands.

It was the first move away from the traditional washing powder and customers loved it.

Ours was produced by a factory in Northern Ireland so I celebrated in style with the manufacturer's managing director at top Mayfair restaurant Le Gavroche run by legendary Roux Brothers Albert and Michel.

It was so exclusive the King and Queen of Sweden were sitting on the next table.

The restaurant also had a tie rack, a cravat rack and a bow-tie rack for diners who arrived minus the appropriate neckwear. No neckwear, no food, no argument.

After a great meal and quite a few drinks my dining companion had to catch a flight back to Northern Ireland early in the afternoon so I decided to go and have a nosey at Christie's Auction house in London.

As luck would have it a load of Lord of the Manor titles were being sold by the Savile Estate in the Huddersfield area and I was already in a giddy, excitable mood so, on the spur of the moment, decided to buy around 10 for around £5,000 each – such as Lord of the Manor of Slaithwaite. I paid £6,500 for Lordship of Greetland, a title dating back to 1086 – that's just 20 years after King Harold's unfortunate demise at the Battle of Hastings and the Norman invasion of England.

I can't remember what they all were but when I'd sobered up and got back home I started to wonder what to do with them all. Then I had a brainwave. The Americans love anything to do with English history and culture so surely they'd be well up for buying a title to become lord of a manor.

I advertised nine of them in the *New York Times* and sold them for $10,000 each. They snapped them up – I just wished I'd bought more. It didn't give them the right to call themselves Lord so and so – I couldn't be Lord Graham – they could just put Lord of the Manor after their name.

So the lords of the manor for many places in the Yorkshire area are Americans who may never have visited our shores.

I kept just one for myself – Lord of the Manor of Greetland.

Why? Well, it was item 13 in the catalogue and I loved the Andy Thornton architectural antiques mill there and the Blue Ball restaurant which was in nearby Norland. It also gave me the right to dance around the Greetland village maypole on May 1.

So I'm still Lord of the Manor of Greetland, although I've yet to dance around the maypole.

But never say never.

Businesses I'm helping now and future plans

Huddersfield has a couple of great music venues, the Parish pub on Queen Street in the town centre and Smile Bar and Venue on Wakefield Road in Aspley. I've helped both to keep moving the businesses forward to try to get people continually coming in. Live entertainment, especially music, is so important and we all need to do what we can to support it.

By the way, if you love country and western music you won't find a better spot than The Tavern in Holmfirth run by Chris Gray.

I love Yorkshire and have this idea to really promote the county's brands by setting up a museum called Yorkshire Global Brands which looks at the history and heritage of the best ones – textiles, engineering, food and drink – and also showcasing the up-and-coming ones.

But it would be a museum like no other … it would be a virtual reality one. Ideally based at the University of Huddersfield, visitors would simply put on a virtual reality headset and be taken on a dramatic tour of the county. Research has already started into this.

One plan I've been working on for a while is Rock Properties.Ltd and with this we aim to transform part of an old RAF training base at Manby in Lincolnshire into a retirement village.

The main building is Tedder Hall, a Grade II listed former RAF teaching building built in 1937, but the place is now abandoned and derelict so our plans would bring new life to it and considerable investment into that part of the county. We have planning permission for 80 properties on the site – mainly apartments in the old buildings including the officers' mess – but ideally we'd need 160 properties. The project is called Beech Grove.

My interest in pharmaceuticals and shaking up the market never diminishes and we've a new product due to be licensed in the summer of 2024.

Myself, son Craig, and Ray Myers who worked with me for many years at Galpharm, set up a company called Pilz Ltd in 2016 which has some great new pharmaceutical products under development.

I've done some voluntary work for a company called Pivot Group which helps youngsters struggling with mainstream schooling in West Yorkshire.

I've gone in to give talks and advice, usually turning up in the Ferrari to grab their attention and interest, even taking them for a spin in it.

It means they're then keen to know how I'd managed to be able to afford the car so they'll really listen. It's all about inspiring and when they learn about my dyslexia it strikes even more of a chord with several of them. I think it helps them to think about their own issues, anxieties and frustrations and encourages them to have hope in life.

It would be great to see this business expand so it can have more of an impact nationally.

I'm now working with Sam Teale, a brilliant young award-winning videographer from Cleckheaton who creates the most magical, modern and emotive videos. One he made about love, loss and poverty at Christmas 2022 called *The Go-Kart* went viral and received more than 40 million views from over 120 countries.

His 2023 video about the impact cancer has on lives was just as powerful, raising money for children's charity Candlelighters and notching up millions of views.

They are, in my opinion, way better than the John Lewis Christmas adverts that get so much hype.

Check out his work on his website called Sam Teale Productions.

I'm keen to give promising new businesses a hand which reminds me of something which happened many years ago.

We were staying at Runswick Bay in North Yorkshire and there had been a terrible storm one night. When we got up in the morning and went to the beach we saw that thousands of starfish had been washed ashore by the crashing waves.

The sun was starting to come up which meant the starfish would quickly perish but in the distance I spotted a lone fisherman picking the starfish up and placing them back in the sea. I went to help and was starting to put some of the starfish back into the water when a dog walker ambled up.

He said to the fisherman: "What are you doing?"

The fisherman replied: "I'm placing the starfish back into the sea otherwise they'll be scorched by the sun."

The dog walker said: "Well, there's thousands of them. What difference will it make?"

The fisherman gently put two more starfish into the sea, turned to the dog walker and said: "Well, it made a difference to them."

I thought it was so poignant and a reflection of life itself, helping people to set off in business and start their careers. So don't pass any starfish in life, always give them a chance if you can.

Why everyone should help charities ... and how charities can help themselves

I've been involved in charities all my adult life and the more you help them, the more you realise why they are so important to so many people. They are at the very heart of our society – life simply wouldn't function without them – with some incredible ones run by people who dedicate their lives to helping others.

So that's why I'd say to everyone to help at least one charity every month, even if it's just setting up a small monthly direct debit to them.

But charities also need to sometimes think differently too. Many simply ask businesses for donations or raffle prizes but in an economic crisis money has never been tighter for everyone.

More valuable than simply writing a cheque would be for business experts to go in and look at the charity, how the organisation operates, ways it could save money in its running costs and how it could find or exploit potential new income streams. Running any organisation is ultimately about profit and loss. Spotting how to change that is one thing but actually implementing it takes wisdom, knowledge and experience.

Many charities are approaching businesses that may already be struggling financially so perhaps the charities need to think about how they can help the businesses in return. That may be going in and giving inspirational talks or coming up with ways the business could meet its corporate social responsibility targets.

I know of a couple with a severely disabled young son who gave a talk to a group of medical students about caring for such a chronically ill child and its impact on them, the rest of their family and how society as a whole viewed disability. By the end, several of the students were in tears. The couple had talked about challenges in such an open, honest and emotional way, that that hour probably stayed with the students forever and gave them a whole new outlook on what working in the NHS actually means.

I was involved helping a kidney charity a few years ago and at a fundraising dinner attended by businesses I was auctioned off to go into the company that paid the highest amount to the charity for my services. My unique selling point was that I'd show them how to double their profits in 12 months.

The company that 'won' me for the day for £3,000 was a family firm of financial advisors run by a dad with his son and daughter. As soon as I walked through the door the son said it was a waste of time and they had more important things to do that day. His father wasn't put off though, so I did a full SWOT analysis of the company in the morning and drew up a plan of action for them in the afternoon. For those who aren't involved in business management, SWOT stands for strengths, weaknesses, opportunities and threats.

One of my suggestions was that the son should leave as he clearly wasn't happy in the business, promote the daughter who had the ability to do more in the company and for the dad to retire as he'd earned it after establishing and running such a good business for so long.

The first charity I was involved in was Holmfirth Round Table in the early 1980s after my solicitor at the time, Paul Brown, invited me to join – an invitation I felt I couldn't refuse.

The charity is for men aged 18 to 45 and it meant on Sundays I picked up old folk from retirement homes and took them to a restaurant in a village near Holmfirth called Holmbridge for a free Sunday lunch paid for by the Round Table.

The Tablers also organised charity football and cricket days but probably their greatest feat was the Holmfirth Duck Race with thousands of the bright yellow little plastic ducks tipped into the River Holme from a digger in the centre of Holmfirth and the first one to reach the Sands playing fields downstream was the winner.

The first race was in July 1984 and it's still going strong, so much so it's now known worldwide. In 2023 it cost £2 to buy a duck with the first past the post winning its owner £1,000. I reckon that's way better odds than the National Lottery.

A few people have asked me if I ever joined the Freemasons or was tempted to do so. Well, my father, Hugh, came across them in Middlesbrough and was so distrustful of their secrecy and not allowing women to join he even tried to get them banned as an illegal organisation and kept pestering the Government to take action.

So, apparently, we Hugh Leslies are banned from joining anyway.

A charity that really aligned with my business was the Prince's Trust. Peter Branson was the Trust's regional director in Yorkshire from 2004 to 2010 and he encouraged me to do some mentoring for young people involved with the Trust setting off in business and I did all I could to give them belief in themselves.

Peter wanted me to become the first ambassador for the Prince's Trust in Yorkshire and made the appointment but apparently landed himself in hot water as he hadn't followed the usual protocols. The important thing was that it meant I could promote the charity and how it worked at business events – something I was very keen to do.

The Trust gave young people grants to help set them up in business which was absolutely vital as many didn't even have a bank account and would struggle to even get one. Many came from very deprived backgrounds while others had served time in prison or battled against drugs and drink.

I also got the young people to talk to businesses about how the Trust had helped them. Those powerful human interest stories and moving firsthand accounts were so much more compelling than me talking about them.

It's action that counts when setting up businesses and the Trust has helped more than one million young people since it was set up with three out of every four it's helped over the last five years finding work, education or training.

Peter Branson became chief executive of the Forget Me Not Children's Hospice in Huddersfield in August 2010 and led it to fantastic success, overseeing the hospice being built and opening in 2013.

His record of achievement is highly impressive and in the eight years he was there grew it from a £400,000 a year operation to £5.2m, from 6 staff to 150 and from zero to 450 children and families being supported. He also set up a hospice at home service. It was and still is rated Outstanding by the Care Quality Commission, putting Forget Me Not in the top 1% of organisations inspected.

Seeing it in action and how it helps children with terminal or life-limiting conditions can be overwhelming which is why I volunteered to get the message about the wonderful work they do out to the business community.

But when it comes to charity my best moment was a load of balls ... literally.

The idea popped into my head when I realised ladies would talk to their best friends about anything, especially if they had a serious illness such as breast cancer.

But with men it's a very different matter with many loath to discuss anything they deemed too personal which could be mental health through to cancer in embarrassing places – no more so than testicular cancer.

So I wondered how I could get men talking about testicular cancer, the importance of discussing it with friends and doing regular checks while raising money for research into testicular cancer at the same time.

The result was the Ball of Balls which began in about 2008 – big events at the Galpharm Stadium raising money and, perhaps even more importantly, raising awareness.

It worked. At the second one I was standing at the urinal with a business leader next to me.

He turned to me and said: "I love you, Graham."

Even I was speechless for a moment. Could it get any more compromising with both of us stood there, flies down.

But, thankfully, he followed it up with: "I love what you've done getting people talking about cancer. I've had testicular cancer and had a ball removed yet never told a soul."

Well, he certainly picked his moment to start talking about it.

The concept behind the Ball of Balls was to auction off balls ... lots of them. By that I mean sports balls ranging from golf balls to football and rugby balls.

Tiger Woods signed one of the golf balls and top England players put their moniker on footballs.

We had three Ball of Balls in all and needed to get as much money from the auction at each one so I had an idea to get the whole room talking to one another. With the seating plan I'd put people next to their friends but also made sure a couple of people they knew were on a neighbouring table. This means they'd be sure to turn round and chat to them and that would be the same for every table so once the meal was underway and the drink was flowing there'd be a real buzz.

And when we got to the auction they'd be urging one another to keep bidding for something. I seem to remember the first ball raising £22,000 and we are now hoping to bring it back to the John Smith's Stadium in 2024.

Wouldn't it be great if all 92 football clubs held at least one event a year to raise awareness about testicular cancer? That really would spread the message far and wide.

There is a saying that charity begins at home, meaning that people should deal with the needs of those close to them before they think about helping others.

I'm not so sure. Yes, family is all-important and the Leslie family is a very close-knit one, but no matter what trials and tribulations everyone faces in life there is always someone worse off than you ... someone who may need the help and support you can give.

Someone you don't even know.

What family means to me

I can deal with most emergencies and crises ... unless it involves my own family.

Then it can be tougher.

When my first wife, Sandra, went into labour and our first child, Craig, was born, I passed out. I came round to find a midwife caring for Sandra and two nurses trying to help me.

When Alex was born many years later I was called into the room to try to support my second wife, Ann, but clearly things weren't going to plan by the look on the staff's faces. There was so much blood it was like carnage in there and the baby's head wasn't even showing.

The staff called for a doctor and in came one who'd previously served in the army. He immediately took control by reaching in and discovered the umbilical cord was around Alex's neck, strangling him. With a quick flick he freed it and Alex's head came out quickly followed by the rest of him. If the doctor hadn't acted so skilfully and decisively Alex may not have survived.

I was so thankful I hugged him, leaving him in shock and me covered in blood.

Fortunately there were no such dramas when my two daughters Amanda and Fay were born.

As a dyslexic parent my children had some unusual – well, downright bizarre – bedtime book experiences. Mary didn't just have a little lamb, she also had pigs and cows as I just embellished books when I struggled to read words or my eye would skip them.

If Jack and Jill went up the hill I'd want to know why on earth they were going up there rather than read that it was something to do with a pail of water.

When it comes to supporting new businesses there's nothing like giving support to family.

It began with me helping a former Co-op marketing director who had a new concept for a rural community petrol station ... combining it with a delicatessen.

He left the business when it became clear we didn't share the same values, but my wife, Karen's son Tom Brooke, had just graduated with a business studies degree and was eager for his first challenge in the commercial world. He renamed the business Brooke's and has the original on the A19 at Shipton by Beningbrough and another on Darlington Road at Richmond.

I used my pension scheme to buy the properties and then rent them to Tom and stood as his guarantor, but he's driven the businesses forward and their annual sales now top £3m a year with profits doubling over the past 12 months.

So stop for fuel and you have the chance to buy single Yorkshire malt whisky, rhubarb gin or cream liqueur alongside beers, ciders and sauces – all from God's own county. They even do an appetite-whetting charcuterie board.

I had a small Hunter sailing boat around 40 years ago which we used to sail off the west coast of Scotland at Largs where my parents lived.

It was in purple and green – my favourite colours – so was easy to spot. I decided to take my two children at the time, Craig and Amanda, to sail around the Isle of Cumbrae just offshore, but I committed the cardinal and unforgiveable sin of not checking the weather forecast first.

Craig would have been about 12 at the time and decided at the last minute he didn't want to go so got off at Largs and went to his grandparents' house. Amanda would be about 10 and was up for the adventure but unfortunately it turned out to be a terrifying one for both of us.

As we sailed round the west coast of the island a storm brewed up with waves quickly crashing over the boat so I made the sails smaller and tried to get the engine started so we could quickly get into the nearest harbour. Unfortunately the engine had been swamped by the seawater and wouldn't go, but I somehow managed to sail round to the south of the island to its only town, Millport.

I took the quickest route to head for the harbour but noticed the white horses of the waves in front of me which indicated we were close to very shallow waters. The boat's keel was around 3.5ft below the surface which meant there was a very real and imminent danger the boat would ground, roll over and both Amanda and me would be lost to the sea.

So I turned around and headed back out to sea and the relative safety of the deeper water despite the storm and managed to finally reach the harbour another way.

I daren't tell Amanda how close we had been to catastrophe until she was about 20. It just shows how things can quickly turn to disaster if you've not prepared properly for them.

My mum, Anne, needed carers for the last four years of her life before we lost her on January 27, 2006, aged 89. As she found it increasingly tougher to go to church, shop and do her daily household chores she applied to Kirklees Council for help from carers.

The staff kept changing and, after a couple of falls, Mum decided to try a nursing home, but only lasted a night before insisting on going back to her own house.

She was far more content there and then a young lady employed by the council became her main carer. Mum loved this carer who she affectionately called 'the wee lassie' and it got me thinking. After chatting to the carer I discovered she was a single mum only earning around £13,000 a year and, for that, she was regularly visiting 10 people a day and paying for her own petrol.

I offered her £10,000 a year to look after my mum and knew two friends in similar situations with ageing parents so they also paid her £10,000 each. So that was just three clients yet she was earning three times more because she was doing such a great job for them and could give each more time.

It meant she had a better lifestyle for herself and her daughter and the last I heard she had set up her own care company and was taking on employees.

Comedienne Catherine Tate once said she'd marry me – well, kind of.

There is a teenage cancer charity in Huddersfield set up in memory of 17-year-old Laura Crane who died from cancer while studying for her A-levels at Greenhead College in the town.

It was called The Laura Crane Trust for many years – recently renamed Project Youth Cancer – and raises money to support medical and social research into cancers that affect young people aged 13 to 24.

In 2007 I was involved in promoting the 11th annual fundraising ball and that year it was a Hollywood theme.

Catherine is the charity's patron but she couldn't attend as she was away filming *Dr Who* with David Tennant so I became auctioneer for the night, trying to persuade people to part with their cash. The auction raised £8,368 with the whole evening bringing in more than £25,000.

When Catherine and David appeared on screen with a really funny pre-recorded message she said it had been mentioned to her that I'd been married three times. Catherine suggested she could have been number four if she'd been there.

Karen was there with me so I wasn't available. Sorry, Catherine.

From Austin 10 to racing around Le Mans in a brand-new Bentley

I've always loved cars since my dad introduced me to his passion for motoring.

There's just something about them that fascinates me and I must have owned 30 to 40 during my life, starting with an old baby Austin 10 and going right up to racing Ferraris and owning Rolls Royces. How lucky was I?

The Austin 10 was at a time when you could have any colour of car you wanted so long as it was black.

But I'd been behind a wheel before I was 17, driving tractors helping friends harvest the fields near where we lived in Middlesbrough and mucking out the stables for rich kids.

On my 17th birthday Dad told me to jump in his Ford Popular and he started to teach me how to drive. It was a manual three-gear engine box and I set off and went straight through the gears without any need for instruction. We hadn't got to the end of Malvern Drive where we lived at number 85 before Dad pulled me over.

"How long have you been driving?" he asked, clearly shocked.

"A couple of years," I replied, quickly adding. "But just tractors helping mates out in the fields."

The first test I took though was my motorbike one on my James 150cc which you could take at 16 and at that time you were sent on a circular course around a few roads with the instructor popping up on street corners to observe and give instructions about what he wanted you to do next.

It was going well until a bloke reversed out of his drive without looking, went straight into me and knocked me off. The bike's front forks were bent which made it too damaged to ride so I picked it up and wheeled it back to the instructor.

"That was going really well until then," he said, cheerily. "But I'm afraid I'll have to fail you."

"Why?" I asked, totally dejected.

"Well, you've not completed the course," he replied.

Apparently pushing the bike round didn't count.

As I'd been riding a bike off road since I was 12 I carried on and we always rode two up anyway with such confidence L-plates were rarely checked. In those days there was no limit on cc size and no law on helmets so off we went thinking we were born free.

Of course, it all ended in tragedy. We were riding back from the coast one night when one of our biking gang was hit by a lorry and we had to identify him in hospital. The only part of his body that I saw had a huge tyre mark across it.

I sold my bike the next day, never to ride again until I passed my test at 55 and, during a mid-life crisis, bought a Harley Davidson.

In a way I believe it'd be good if everyone had a go at riding a motorbike at some point as it teaches the importance of tyres and brakes. With so little rubber in contact with the road and the need to be careful braking, especially in the wet, if you make a mistake then you're thrown off the machine. Make a mistake in a car and you'll end up having a bump and probably walk away, which is why so many car drivers are so blasé about speed and braking. They don't know the dangers and repercussions until it's too late.

Even now if it's snowy or icy I'll deliberately skid or do a handbrake turn in an empty car park to test my driving skills and how I'd get out of it should the worst happen and I lose control on the roads.

The good news was I passed my car test first time so had the freedom to drive my dad into work every day.

I had been taught by an ex-police driving instructor in Dad's Ford Anglia – I can even remember its registration number was WTN 695 – who had high standards. He'd pop a saucer of water on the dashboard and if I juddered the car setting off, the water would spill and he'd tell me I'd failed.

For hill starts he'd get out, pop a box of matches right behind the back wheel and if I rolled over them, I'd fail. That's probably why I passed as the driving test examiner's standards were far less severe.

A week before my test my dad took me to London to drive there and boost my confidence. I suppose if you can drive in London you can drive anywhere. Boy, did it work.

As an inquisitive teenager me and friends would strip cars down to try to make them go faster and at one point we even took all the doors off one to see if it would make it go any quicker. It did but we discovered the journey was far breezier, colder and more dangerous.

Someone introduced us to the cut and thrust of stock car racing, so we entered a car into a race and had the brilliant idea to fill the door panels with concrete to make it more robust every time someone smashed into it. Unfortunately it meant we could only go half the speed so were a sitting duck in the demolition derby.

Better innovation came later in my career, but it usually does after a few unsuccessful attempts, yet you keep on trying.

After I moved to Huddersfield I met a car dealer called Lou Lomax and he got me into buying and selling cars and I ended up with an Arthur Daley style car sales plot next to my fledgling Galpharm businesses when I first set up in the early 1980s.

I'd usually buy the cars from Brighouse Car Auctions, drive them for a month or so and then sell them. They were often Mercedes or Jaguars so I quickly got used to the more upmarket motors which eventually led me to the crossroads car choice. Anyone lucky enough to be able to select their next level of car either goes for a Porsche or a Ferrari.

I went Ferrari and have stuck with them ever since.

My first one in the 1990s was serviced by John Pogson, owner of a company called Italia Autosport in Meltham near Huddersfield and he suggested we raced Ferraris on what's known as the Maranello Challenge, a series of races for Ferrari owners around the UK sponsored by its main importer in London, Maranello. I love speed and so the natural step was to go into motor racing.

First I needed a racing car and spotted a Ferrari 308 for sale with the number plate Who 308. Intrigued, I inquired and discovered it was being sold by Roger Daltrey from The Who and he actually popped into the Galpharm headquarters at Dodworth near Barnsley with the paperwork. Unfortunately I was out, but a few days later the phone rang in the office and switchboard said it was a Roger Daltrey on the line.

Now, I was often playing pranks with friends phoning them up and pretending to be someone else – I did particularly good Sean Connery, Ted Heath and Tommy Cooper impersonations – so immediately thought this was one of my victims getting their own back.

So when I answered I was on the front foot, asking: "Right then, come on, who's trying to have me on. I'm not falling for this."

The voice on the other end of the line said slowly and with precision: "It is Roger Daltrey. I want to talk to you about the car you've just bought from me."

"Give over," I said. "Is that you, Dave?"

But then he said something about the car only he would know. I felt so stupid.

Yes, it was him and he insisted I made sure the registration plate always stayed with the car, even if I eventually sold it.

I assured him it would and it did when I did sell it.

Thirteen is my lucky number even though most people shun it like the plague. It was my dad's birthday and I suppose having such an unloved number as my favourite one is just another part of why I seem to think differently. People say I'm like a crab going in a divergent direction to everyone else.

Incidentally, Meltham was the home of the famous David Brown Tractors factory founded by tycoon David Brown who also owned the Aston Martin company, put his initials on the Aston Martin DB6 in the 1960s and the Aston Martin then became synonymous with James Bond.

I needed a race licence to race the Ferrari in the Maranello Challenge and it was made clear that if any driver did anything really stupid they'd not be allowed to race again.

We competed at race tracks countrywide including Brands Hatch in Kent, Snetterton in Norfolk, Oulton Park in Cheshire and Donington Park in Leicestershire, regularly reaching speeds of 130mph.

I won several races in my category and someone must have been watching as I was contacted by a Bentley dealership in Sheffield to say the company was launching a new model called the Bentley Arnage named after the famous Arnage bends on the Le Mans circuit in northwest France. It was 1998 and this car was powered by a new, all-aluminium V8 engine and twin turbochargers.

To mark the occasion they were flying in potential customers from around the world and did I want to drive some of the people from the UK around the circuit?

If there was ever an offer I couldn't refuse it was this and they even flew me to the race track in a private jet where I was met by a guy called Stuart. He took me round the course in a brand-new Bentley Arnage – there was a whole fleet of 40 there – and taught me just how to drive through the Arnage S-bends the quickest I possibly could and exactly where to accelerate.

He did this because there was a competition for the driver who could negotiate the bends the quickest the next day when the potential customers were being driven around the track.

It made me nervous. Last thing I wanted to do was to go off-piste with a £145,000 Bentley, damaging the car, myself and the customer.

On the day itself Stuart came up with some cracking advice.

"When you get to Arnage, just boot it," he said.

So I followed his words of wisdom without easing off at all or touching the brakes and made it round the bends OK every time.

In the evening there was a wining and dining celebration in a marquee when the master of ceremonies made a great play of revealing who was the fastest through the Arnage bends.

The winner was a Frenchman in 11.2 seconds, I came second in 11.7 seconds with the German driver sitting next to me third in 12.1 seconds.

The MC held up a hand as the applause died down.

"Ladies and gentlemen, we have a surprise for you," he said, creating a sense of drama. "We asked Formula One racing driver Nigel Mansell to drive a Bentley through Arnage too."

And in stepped the great man himself to rapturous applause. After all, he was a massive name in Formula One at the time and had won the world title in 1992.

The MC then revealed Nigel's time through the Arnage ... 7.4 seconds."

The applause got even louder.

It showed the difference between a decent amateur racing driver and a real professional at the top of his game.

The German looked at me and said with a shake of his head: "Do you realise that if we were racing Nigel Mansell at Le Mans he'd lap us on the third lap."

It put my driving prowess well and truly into perspective.

Bentley continued with the Arnage until 2010 when it was replaced by the Mulsanne.

Car racing can be a dangerous sport, especially at an amateur level.

I was racing the Ferrari 308 around Snetterton in the Maranello Challenge and had just overtaken another car before going into a bend followed by a chicane. As I looked in my mirror the driver of the car I'd just overtaken was trying so hard to catch up he lost control, the car spun and then rolled over. It looked bad.

The race was immediately stopped and the driver, a young man in his 20s, was taken to hospital with very serious injuries. Sadly, he didn't make it.

I was about 50 at the time and after that tragedy my children started to tell me I was too old to be taking part in car racing. I think they were right and stopped not long after.

My love of nature and art

One of the first products we had made under the Galpharm name was sweeteners but at that time they all came in a round tubular dispenser.

I wanted something different and main brand Canderel were going for different shapes. I was on the beach at Runswick Bay in North Yorkshire and loved to feel the smooth pebbles, which gave me an idea for a totally different shape dispenser would be a great marketing ploy.

I brought six back with me – all different shapes – and asked Galpharm staff which they felt was the smoothest to touch and carry, the most comfortable in their hands.

One was chosen which I took to the mould manufacturer. He looked at it, rolled it over in his hand, mulled it over for a few minutes and then said: "Most people come with a drawing."

"Nature chose it," I replied. And that became the product's logo.

It was wonderful for staff morale as they played a part in the decision-making process and the sweetener became a national success because of its great shape with stores then wanting it for their own brands. Another winner.

It just shows that nature can often have the answers when you're searching for inspiration. You just need to go out there and look with an open mind.

When I was punished at school – often for not reading properly – I had to stand outside the classroom, but there were three bushes in the quadrangle and birds were always nesting there.

My mum later told the teacher at a parents' evening: "Graham seems to know more about birds than he does about English and maths."

That love of nature still remains. I often sit outside on the patio at home on an evening thinking and just enjoying the sights and sounds of nature. It can be all-immersive, so peaceful and relaxing and there's no bigger connection than making a human connection with nature.

I found a young crow recently that had been abandoned by its mother. I fed it milk, seed and bread for a couple of nights and on the third night it flew over and sat on my arm.

That's a very special connection.

I also love art and the immense skill and creativity it involves never ceases to amaze and inspire me. I probably got that from my mum who sketched and painted later in life.

I met Mirfield-based Richard Gower a few years ago when he was doing art alongside his day job as a graphic designer for some big store brands. He's brilliantly talented but really wanted to concentrate just on his art and has now dropped the graphic design.

We met regularly to think of ways to drive his name and business forward and one of the ideas has been to not just sell the artwork, but also the palette he's used to create it as he uses a new one for every commission. People can then grasp the scale of the journey that artwork has made from those few colours on a palette to a magnificent piece of art they'll admire forever. A framed palette also looks pretty good.

Richard also signs his artwork in a very unique way. Every original has half a dollar fixed to the back of it and Richard has the other half. A dollar note has two identical serial numbers on the front so Richard has one of them and the buyer has the other.

He's so talented and can paint in any style from Picasso to Van Gogh. More recently he's done a painting of a photo of legendary former Huddersfield Town manager Neil Warnock walking down a corridor in the club and we've sold limited edition prints of it to raise money for charity.

He also did one of Huddersfield Town centre back Christopher Schindler scoring the winning penalty at Wembley to send Town into the Premier League in 2017.

Richard painted Schindler taking the spot kick and did a limited edition of 50 which raised thousands of pounds for The Leslie Sports Foundation and Huddersfield Town Foundation charities.

Richard did a painting depicting the Duke of Edinburgh's last ever formal engagement in August 2017 meeting Royal Marines at Buckingham Palace who had done a 1,664-mile trek for charity. This was in his role as their Captain General and the painting captures the poignant moment he tipped his bowler hat to them.

I suggested he send it to the Queen and he wrote to Her Majesty offering the painting as a gift. Richard received a letter back from the Queen's Lady In Waiting saying that throughout the Queen's reign she had never accepted a painting from any artist as they had all been commissioned.

However, she added that if Richard would like to go to Buckingham Palace the Queen would graciously receive the gift. He did and so, it seems, Richard is the only artist to have provided the Queen with a painting that wasn't commissioned.

Another great moment was meeting LS Lowry ... in a classroom at Upperthong Junior and Infant School in Holmfirth.

The headteacher at the time was a lady called Margaret Douglas. This would have been in the early 1970s and she'd somehow persuaded Lowry to go and give a talk to the pupils.

I asked if I could go and sit at the back and she let me. It was awe-inspiring listening to him talk about his matchstick men, but not a lot of people realise that Lowry was a classically trained artist, so had a far greater artistic range and skill than people credit him for with people only remembering him for his matchstick work.

His work is on permanent display at the Lowry in Salford and is well worth a visit.

I also have pictures from Huddersfield artist Joseph O'Reilly who is brilliant at still life and I continue to be an avid collector of his work.

I first met him while busking in Huddersfield town centre in the 1970s when he was doing sketches on the pavement as a street artist. It began to rain so I packed my gear up and started to walk away when I noticed his drawings were being washed away.

I asked him how he could put up with seeing such great work simply disappearing before his eyes and he simply replied: "That's the way it is."

It always left an impression on me and years later I saw one of his paintings at Holmfirth Art Exhibition of a tuxedo jacket slung over a chair with the sun coming in through the window. It was remarkable and I really wanted it, but it had already been sold.

Still, I've ended up with lots more and they are all up my staircase so every night is a wonderful walk up to bed.

Little drummer boy ends up taking music to a global level

I've always loved music but it really started when I began playing the snare drum in the Boys' Brigade Company No 2 in Middlesbrough at the age of 12 and quickly became lead drummer on the parades through the town's streets.

My parents obviously weren't that enamoured with my choice of noisy instrument but luckily there was a field at the end of our street – Malvern Drive in Brookfield – so I was banished there to practise.

It was fine during the summer months as I did my paradiddle roll complete with putting the drumsticks smartly up to my nostrils each time, but when the farmer ploughed the field it became a lot trickier. The deep furrows then meant I wasn't walking straight with one leg higher than the other but the band leader had the perfect solution. He told me to march at the kerbside with one leg on the kerb and the other on the road so I'd be mirroring what it's like in the field. Not the best of solutions, really.

By 1962 I'd progressed to be lead singer of the band The Defenders covering the likes of Cliff Richard, Adam Faith and Buddy Holly. We were young and keen and it helped that the drummer's dad was caretaker at Park End School in Middlesbrough and let us practise there so as not to disturb anyone else's peace and quiet.

Best gig we ever played was at the impressive landmark Coatham Hotel in Redcar, which was home to Redcar Jazz Club from 1960 with top musicians appearing there such as Ronnie Scott, Cleo Laine, Acker Bilk, Kenny Ball, Rod Stewart, Chris Rea, Eric Clapton, Mark Bolan, Long John Baldry, Roger Daltrey, Keith Moon, Pete Townshend, Georgie Fame, Alan Price and Joe Cocker. That's an impressive line-up by any standards.

But we normally played working men's clubs which were an eye-opener in many ways. I'll never forget a working men's club in Redcar one Sunday lunchtime where we were standing waiting in the wings while the MC made the introductions.

He said: "We've got a young band for you today, ladies and gentleman. But first, please put your hands together for the stripper."

On she came, Susie her name, off came her clothes and we stood there with eyes wide and mouths open. We'd never seen a woman naked before, let alone a stripper. Even stranger, the audience carried on talking to one another as if she wasn't there. It was a bizarre, almost surreal experience.

Then it was our turn. Our first song was Adam Faith's hit 'What Do You Want?' and some wag shouted out, 'Bring the stripper back on.'

The MC was straight back on the microphone again: "Pie and peas are just about to be served at the back."

The audience surged as one to the back of the venue to queue up for the pies and peas and we were left playing to empty seats.

The next show was at Kirklevington Country Club near Yarm where Long John Baldry, the man who later discovered Rod Stewart busking at Twickenham Railway Station, was singing.

But that gig signalled the end of my early rock career.

A huge musical talent in the Leslie family is my brother, Hugh, who played the piano and loved it so much he studied to be a concert pianist at the Guildhall School of Music.

My sister Annette was also a star piano player who passed her grade 8 when she was still very young.

My dad's interest in music was purely classical, but during the war he was a member of the All India Gramophone Society which played classical music on gramophone records in Delhi every Sunday in 1943 and 1944. He always loved his classical music and singers such as Paul Robeson, Al Johnson and Mario Lanza.

I didn't really get into music again until I landed in Huddersfield in 1971 when I ended up living alone after my divorce in the mid-70s. I bought a classic guitar for £1.50 from a second-hand shop and taught myself how to play so I could descend into hazy, bluesy, boozy music moments all by myself, which was the title of a smash hit but sadly not mine.

By 1976 I had around a dozen songs in my repertoire – those I could play on the guitar and sing – and even did a gig playing to children in hospital at Christmas. It made me realise how much I was missing my own children so went home and wrote a song called 'Travelling Home for Christmas' – a full 10 years before Chris Rea had his huge hit with 'Driving Home for Christmas'.

There's another link there as Chris was part of the well-known Rea family in Middlesbrough who ran ice-cream and coffee shops in the North East and I used to cut their hair in my hairdressing days, including Chris's when he was around 10 years old.

I simply had no time for music during the Galpharm years but came back to it when Hugh retired and moved back up north to Huddersfield from London in June 2016.

He'd helped me before though. I'd composed a love song for Karen for our marriage in 2011 at Ripon Cathedral called 'I Will Love You (Wedding Song)' based on Pachelbel's Canon in D, but needed Hugh's musical expertise to develop and arrange the song so it could be sung by a choir during the ceremony, as a wedding march as we left the cathedral and later as a string trio at the reception. That was unbelievably emotional for me, hearing my song being played by the cathedral's organ as we left the church.

Hugh discovered I'd written quite a few songs – what he kindly called 'musical sketches' – and helped me to turn them into something using his phenomenal musical knowledge.

He now lives in an area of Huddersfield called Almondbury where he has a small recording studio known as Studio 111 in his home and is affectionately known by the locals as FILTH – Failed In London Try Huddersfield.

I was introduced to songwriter and producer Eliot Kennedy after Karen bought his house in the Holme Valley. Eliot has a brilliant music CV having written the Spice Girls' first global hit 'Say You'll Be There' and also written and produced for Celine Dion, Boyzone, Blue, S Club 7, Five, Billie Piper, Atomic Kitten and Bryan Adams.

He also formed a songwriting partnership with Gary Barlow. In 1993 Eliot co-wrote and co-produced songs on Take That's second album *Everything Changes* and, together with Gary, they wrote the songs for the musicals *Finding Neverland* and *Around the World in Eighty Days*.

I'd put together a collection of songs and Eliot agreed to arrange and help me record them which he did for my debut album called *Galbum*. That's my initials Graham Andrew Leslie again, this time with a bum stuck on the end to try to make it sound like album although, in hindsight, I'm not 100% sure that worked, but it's certainly memorable.

Eliot and I did record 'Travelling Home for Christmas' together with a children's choir in 2019 to bring money in for the redevelopment of the cancer and leukaemia ward at Sheffield Children's Hospital and performed it at a Christmas fundraising show there which raised around £10,000. The song's now on Spotify.

In 2018 I was mentoring a company in Huddersfield set up by film director Ben Sweet called Film Buddy which was a way of people learning about the film industry and how it works online to inspire the next generation of film makers.

Ben had made a short film called *All the Way Up* about strange happenings in a lift at the Queens Hotel in Leeds. It was directed by TV star David Jason and won several awards at the Monaco International Film Festival and gained international recognition. The cast included Adrian Dunbar who has played Superintendent Ted Hastings in all six series of BBC Television's *Line of Duty*, and Lee Ingleby, best known as abrasive Detective Sergeant John Bacchus in the BBC TV series *Inspector George Gently* set in the 1960s.

Karen and I have invested in another of Ben's short films called *The Irritant* about four people in a small room dealing with their paranoia and which was filmed in Kirklees Council offices one weekend.

Ben was a friend of Bradford-born composer Benson Taylor who had gone on to have a very successful career in the USA writing music for TV and film and his credits include major TV shows such as *Grey's Anatomy*, *Suits* and *Orange is the New Black*. We met when Ben brought Benson along to a mentoring session I was doing.

Benson had been commissioned by Universal Music to create a $2m state-of-the-art music studios at a converted convent in Tuscany, Italy, and he wanted advice on how to create a business plan and model to buy the convent during lockdown, so I was more than happy to help.

I sent my version of 'Travelling Home for Christmas' to Benson who said he couldn't get it out of his head and so did his own arrangement and recorded it with a session singer which sounded amazing.

Fate then stepped in. Michael Jackson's mother was walking down a corridor at Sony Music in Los Angeles when she heard the track, loved it and was told Benson was looking for a well-known name in the music industry to sing it.

Mrs Jackson certainly had someone in mind, her daughter La Toya Jackson who also immediately loved it and phoned Benson herself to say she wanted to record it as soon as possible in the same studio as Michael had recorded his legendary 'Thriller' track.

La Toya recorded 'Travelling Home for Christmas' in 2020 and it's due to be used in an upcoming film called *The Chelsea Cowboy* charting the life of London gangster John Bindon who was also an actor specialising in playing violent thugs and was acquitted of murder in 1978.

La Toya even sent me an email which said: "I must say 'Travelling Home for Christmas' is such a beautiful song. What a talent. It was my pleasure to sing it. I thank you for writing it."

That certainly was a moment.

Benson makes things happen. I'd written a gospel song called 'United Together'. Benson then did a musical arrangement and thought it would be perfect for the London-based Kingdom Choir which sang at Harry and Meghan's wedding in May 2018 and the King's coronation in 2023.

The choir's leader, Karen Gibson, had been on the radio complaining that people didn't write anthems anymore, which my brother, Hugh, heard and told me and I then told Benson.

The group loved it and Benson organised them to record it at the Abbey Road studios made world-famous by The Beatles. That was done in January 2023. They have since performed it live.

Now, looking to the future, Benson and I have devised a whole new way to get music out to the world. How many musicians are out there writing great tracks and music that would be perfect for films, TV and adverts but simply can't get it heard by anyone.

They end up on Spotify along with at least 28 million other artists and, unless someone knows your name, they wouldn't search for you or download your music. Unless you're out there gigging and working exceptionally hard to get known, then your music – no matter how great it is – usually goes nowhere.

We are working on giving them that global platform through a pioneering way that gives composers a far greater chance of getting their music heard.

We've set up a company called Luco Music Group (lucomusicgroup.com) which has been appointed by the Warner Music Group to represent them in the UK.

Through Luco, Benson's music has appeared on the 2020 film *Chick Fight* starring Malin Akerman, Bella Thorne and Alec Baldwin.

We are looking for musicians who would like their music to be exposed globally to producers of music for films, TV and adverts. They simply upload their music onto our website and we send it on to Warner who then distribute it worldwide, releasing the new music they receive every week. People who want original music for projects can then pay a rental fee or even buy it outright.

Benson and I have worked closely with an IT genius, Simon Milner – one of the world's leading Artificial Intelligence creators and innovators – who has recently returned to his native Huddersfield after 20 years in Los Angeles and now works out of my suite at the 3M Buckley Innovation Centre.

We have brought out an AI App so young musicians can distribute their work globally with Warner Music and we've done that through another company called Luco Labs Ltd.

Having Benson and Simon working together with me is one of those rare times when the stars align when you're trying to be adventurous and creative. It's an electrifying and amazing experience and another world first from West Yorkshire.

I'm also keen to support bands from the past and Magna Carta were a big name in progressive rock in the 1960s and 70s, selling nine million albums and supporting the likes of The Beatles, Jimi Hendrix and David Bowie. I got to know lead singer Chris Simpson when he came into the Woodman Inn at Thunderbridge near Huddersfield, and when I got to know their songs I marvelled at the deep, poetic lyrics. I've now done a deal to secure the rights to their back catalogue and some of their music is in the *Chelsea Cowboy* film.

Chris's lyrics are so good he should have been the original Yorkshire Poet Laureate.

Great quotes and sayings that have inspired me

There's a business saying I really like that's about bacon and egg which says the chicken just turned up while the pig was committed. That sums up some people in business – those who give their absolute all while others stand back and make a token effort.

So here's a list of quotes that inspire me, including some of my own. I hope you make sense of them and they inspire you too.

May I have been in heaven a full hour before the devil knows I'm dead.

Remember, of all the people you meet in life there are only two categories – radiators or drains.

The greatest gift parents can give their children is wings.

I always say that when my sister Annette left Reading University she saw a sign that said Drink Canada Dry ... so she went to give it a go.

Einstein said that only a life lived for others is a life worthwhile.

Never regret anything that makes you laugh.

The greatest risk in life is that you take each other for granted.

It's not what you gather but what you scatter that matters.

Born to do it then die without it.

When I was a lad business was about who you knew, but now it's about who knows you ... yet a combination of both makes a very successful company.

Don't regret your mistakes as regrets are the hardest things to carry as you get older.

The culture to remember in business is to be a speedboat, not a tanker.

If you're one degree off course then correct it or else you'll end up 101 degrees off course.

Never trust anyone who says 'we will never fall out over money'.

Issac Newton said: "If I have seen further it is by standing on the shoulders of Giants."

Theodore Roosevelt said: "The more you know about the past, the better you are prepared for the future."

Always dress for your future role in life, not for the one you currently have.

It's not just about getting a job, it's more important than that. It's about ownership of your life and future.

The five senses of selling, which we all do, are smelling, tasting, hearing, touching and seeing. Everyone sells.

If at first you don't succeed ... move on.

Innovation never sleeps ... neither does money.

My niece, Alice Staveley, is a senior lecturer in English at Stanford University in the USA and loves this quote from author Virginia Woolf: *"I can only note that the past is beautiful because one never realises an emotion at the time. It expands later and thus we don't have complete emotions about the present, only about the past."*

Her husband, Ravi Vakil, is a mathematics professor at Stanford University and has this great quote: *"Time is a construct of the imagination."*

Here's a longer quote I saw in Belize, headlined 'The Fight of Two Wolves Within You':
An old man is teaching his grandson about life.
    "A fight is going on inside me," he said to the boy. "It's a terrible

fight and is between two wolves. One is evil – he is anger, envy, greed and arrogance.

"The other is good – he is joy, peace, love, humility and kindness. The same fight is going on inside you and inside every other person too."

The grandson thought about it for a moment and then asked his grandfather: "Which one will win?"

The old man replied: "The one you feed."

Afterwords

In this final section of the book others have their say on Graham, starting with what his family thinks

Karen Leslie is Graham's third and, he always stresses, his final wife

Karen and her first husband knew Craig Leslie but had never met Graham until her car was parked next to his at Sainsbury's car park at Shorehead in Huddersfield town centre in 2005.

She knew from that first week that Graham could be, well, different.

Karen said: "I'd stayed at a friend's villa in Spain and Graham's name had come up in conversation as he has a villa not far away.

"By sheer coincidence he parked in front of me at Sainsbury's car park the day after we'd flown back and got out of his car wearing his Ugg boots and clutching his man purse.

"I couldn't resist telling him I'd just been near his villa in Spain and he looked at me as though he'd known me all my life and yet he'd never met me before. After a quick chat when he revealed he was off to India on a business trip that night, he gave me his business card and said to give him a call and we'd go out for a drink.

"I was a bit taken aback as I'd recently become single again at the age of 44 with three children and fixed braces on my teeth. Anyway, I sent him a message the next day saying it was nice to meet him and I hoped his trip went all right.

"We kept texting that week. I sent him the latest football scores and he sent me details about his diarrhoea. When he got back I said I was going to a friend's silver wedding and did he want to join me. He did and that was our first date. Graham turned up in his Bentley with a bottle of champagne and a tube of love hearts."

At the time Karen was administrator for Logistics and Hospitality Management at the University of Huddersfield, often travelling to Hong Kong where the university ran courses and helping to create a distance learning diploma for students out there.

She later became a volunteer for West Yorkshire Police, helping the inspector in charge of the police volunteer scheme which saw people in roles as diverse as looking after police dogs and horses through to checking CCTV and tagging evidence. She left in 2012 to create the interior design at The Woodman Inn at Thunderbridge after it had been bought by Craig and Graham.

She reveals that Graham is a true romantic, proposing to her in front of the Taj Mahal in India on one knee. He'd previously bought her a commitment ring as he had no intention of marrying again, but then changed his mind.

The couple married on June 3, 2011, at Ripon Cathedral and Karen did all the wedding planning herself, but adds: "It took months of planning and the day seemed to last the full 24 hours but everyone just seems to remember it for the three-minute song Graham wrote for me."

Karen, who is now Graham's PA as well as his wife, said: "He's always happy and jolly, sometimes irritatingly so, and is forever the joker. You won't find anyone more generous and he's allowed me to be myself throughout our marriage. There is a lot of respect between us.

"One of his great talents is that when he's with someone – and that could be in his business or personal life – he has all the time in the world for them and makes them feel they are the most important person. He gets so much pleasure helping people and setting them off in business.

"He never stops being creative and is always looking for new ideas or potentially innovative products. He hates paperwork and administration which he sees as unproductive and not creative so I sort that out for him.

"Graham is someone who never stops thinking, is always looking for a new challenge and thinks he'll go on forever.

"He is that person who thinks his age is just a number … and one to be ignored."

Annette Staveley is Graham's older sister, and orator and professor of English at the University of Newfoundland and Labrador in Canada, specialising in Victorian and Edwardian British literature

Annette emigrated to Canada in the late 1960s with her husband, Mike, when they won Canadian Scholarships to the University of Alberta and Mike became Professor of Geography and Dean of Arts at the University of Newfoundland and Labrador.

Annette has always remained very close to Graham even though she lives so far away.

She says: "Throughout his life, Graham has wholeheartedly given his time, energy and talents to making life better for others.

"He has demonstrated the positive spirit that sees obstacles as opportunities and difficulties as challenges. His warm and engaging personality is fuelled by his innate and indomitable optimism. He believes 'there is always a way, you just have to keep looking for it.'

"He is little changed from the young boy who was the despair of his parents because he would give away his own few toys to children who had none in Manton Avenue in Middlesbrough in the 1950s.

"Dad, and especially Mum, feared he would be taken advantage of all his life. Maybe he has, but not only has he given joy to many of all ages, he has felt the joy in giving back to the community in which he thrived, against all the odds."

Annette says the bond between herself and younger brothers Graham and Hugh has always been incredibly strong … and that came from their parents.

She says: "We three, as I affectionately call us, have never faltered in our support and love of each other and of our respective families for the 50 years I've lived and worked in Canada. That loyalty, resilience and faith in each other was the firm foundation our mother and father gave us and has lasted all our lives.

"Our parents were stoic, strong and would always tell us not to get above ourselves or be big-headed and to always recognise where we came from and who had helped us along life's way. Mum and Dad had an incredibly strong sense of duty, loyalty and commitment to each other with shared values, a wonder and joy in their companionship and a passionate need for one another.

"They always encouraged us to be independent and supported us in whatever we did but made it clear we would have to live with the consequences of our own decisions.

"I recall their favourite song was 'I'll Walk Beside You' and they did always cherish each other along with Graham, myself and Hugh. It's not for nothing that the Leslie Clan motto is Stand Your Own Ground and Grip Fast."

Annette added: "Whatever they faced in life it was with a sense of wit and irony which may be why Graham is so good at reading people.

"Our dad saw just how unjust, callous, brutal and inhumane life can be during his time in the British army in India and returned determined to dedicate his life to finding ways to combat the darkness in men's and women's hearts and souls. This he did without fear or favour as a probation officer.

"Mum and Dad were a huge protection against the classism, sexism and racial intolerance in England at that time. My parents never put labels on people, they honoured a person's quality of character, not their class or colour and that was well before it was fashionable to hold these views.

"When I began my professional life as a teacher at Kendrick Grammar School in Reading I was soon aware that many students suffered because of neglect and poverty and that it was a teacher's duty to praise and encourage, showing students how to succeed and not to be detached and unfeeling."

Annette was also aware of Graham's dyslexia and how that held him back at school.

"I remember his dyslexia so vividly and was always very protective of him and I still am," she said.

But Graham was always an adventurer with endless curiosity that often got him into scrapes.

Annette said: "One of my early roles in life was to roam the streets of Dagenham looking for Graham. He'd just go off wandering and one day ended up with a serious leg injury needing many stitches after trying to climb over a barbed wire fence. There was blood everywhere and we even feared he could lose his leg it looked that bad."

She added: "Mum was really outgoing, made friends easily and people loved her ... just like Graham. He's the ultimate people person."

Hugh Leslie, Graham's younger brother, is a talented musician and retired lighting hire and sales company director who won a scholarship at the Guildhall School of Music and Drama in London, graduating as an Associate in 1974

Hugh, who has theatre experience in the West End, has worked with Graham on many of his musical projects and says his brother can be something of a maverick when it comes to music.

"Graham's style is eclectic which is normally seen as an insult," said Hugh. "But the true meaning is that he has composed tunes in many different musical genres. He can compose the most intimate song of love and loss and then a stadium rousing anthem for climate change.

"He's rock and roll, he's a balladeer, he's gospel, he sings the blues and he's even country – and the clue to that last genre is in the title of his song 'My Baby Don't Need Nobody All Night Long'.

"He's not a trained musician which means he doesn't always conform to the structure and form a classical musician would expect. He'll bring in chord changes which, on paper, I'd say you can't do that, but when he does they usually end up sounding all right. It makes his compositions interesting, edgy and a pleasure to play.

"His songs have considerable musical merit and people have now taken them on board and are running with them which is why world-famous The Kingdom Choir in London performs his Gospel song 'United Together'.

"I like to see authenticity in an artist and Graham has that in buckets."

Graham is a romantic soul who wrote a song for Karen at their wedding at Ripon Cathedral in 2011 called 'I Will Love You' based on Pachelbel's Canon in D and Hugh helped him with the arrangements so it could be performed by four voices in harmony and a soprano soloist. Hugh helped transform it into a wedding march as the couple left the cathedral and a softer version for a string trio at the reception.

Hugh said: "I'd lived and worked in London for many years and it's only in the last decade or so that we've worked together on music.

"While working on the love song I quickly realised that Graham had a largely untapped musical gift. He had amassed a back catalogue of about 12 original songs. However, these tunes could be a bit chaotic as he'd have a great chorus but no verse, a cracking verse but no chorus and then a verse and a chorus but no lyrics.

"Graham decided that once the songs where completed he would take them into the recording studio. Helped by the multi-award-winning music producer Eliot Kennedy, we ended up with over 20 quality tracks"

Hugh is an experienced pianist but learned the instrument to stop a potential family row.

He said: "In the 1960s we moved into a bungalow but still had our big black piano which took up a lot of space. No-one was playing it and one teatime my dad suddenly announced that he'd arranged for a work colleague to come and collect it. Mum immediately got uppity and told him in no uncertain terms that it had been given to her before they got married and it wasn't his to pass on.

"She also announced that I was starting piano lessons the following Monday. That was a big surprise to Dad and an even more massive shock to me as she'd obviously decided that on the spur of the moment to keep the piano, but I did the lessons for six years with well-known Middlesbrough piano teacher Miss E Redman.

"Mind you, I weaponised that piano. If, for instance, I wasn't allowed to watch television I'd say I had my piano practice to do anyway and then play the same tune again and again and again until my parents could stand it no more, relented and let me do what I wanted.

"But it led me into music where I made so many friends and have had great enjoyment over the years, especially with Graham."

Graham's eldest son Craig worked alongside him at Galpharm for many years and is a very successful businessman in his own right

Graham and Craig forged the perfect partnership at Galpharm with Craig the expert buyer and Graham concentrating on marketing.

Both were driven by a strong desire to sell and beat their competitors but, like any family relationships, it wasn't always plain sailing.

In 1967 Craig was born to Graham and his first wife, Sandra, who he describes as the female version of his dad – flamboyant, great company and a million per cent grafter – but after their divorce in the mid-1970s he didn't spend much time with Graham until they started to work together years later.

After finishing his A-levels at Huddersfield New College, Craig's aim at 17 was to join the Royal Artillery – his grandad's old regiment – and he was offered a commission to train as an officer at Sandhurst.

But Graham desperately didn't want him to join the military, persuaded Craig he had the 'gift of the gab' and would be great at selling so helped get him a job as a trainee salesman at Wilkinson Sword razor company in 1985.

Craig said: "He saw something in me which he does in a lot of people. He's very motivational, inspirational and positive."

Craig loved it at Wilkinson, rose quickly through the ranks to be the company's youngest regional sales rep and then became national sales manager before moving on to Jeyes in a similar role. He was being headhunted by German corporation Vileda when he popped in to see his dad who had just moved Galpharm from Huddersfield to Brighouse.

Craig recalls: "It was a small office and warehouse and I remember there was a lot of paracetamol on pallets. Dad explained what he was doing and how he aimed to sell paracetamol into the big supermarkets.

Working with Wilkinson Sword I knew the potential of own brand products and could see there was a lot of money to be potentially made from medicines in the long-run.

"I had a BMW outside, a well-paid job with a great lifestyle, yet Dad set out persuading me to join Galpharm which then mainly consisted of him, a warehouse guy called Arthur and Pat who worked in the office.

"Within three hours I'd agreed to join him at half my salary, the BMW had to go and my future had suddenly become uncertain. It was a key decision in my life, yet with very little logic behind it.

"Dad being Dad then jetted off to Florida for a couple of weeks so I was left in a cold, empty office wondering what to do next."

Craig quickly got to grips with the business by visiting lots of the buyers in supermarkets he knew from his Wilkinson Sword days and got them very interested in selling their own brand medicines such as paracetamol, aspirin and ibuprofen over the counter.

When he started with Graham the business had a £200,000 a year turnover, but Craig also branched it out into razor blades which he sourced cheaply elsewhere in the world and then did a £1m deal selling Gillette blades into big names such as Morrisons, Superdrug and Lloyds Chemist.

As a buyer with years of experience he could spot fake razor blades a mile off, but while he was away on honeymoon Graham dabbled in buying after finding some Gillette blades at well under the usual market rate which he sold to Morrisons.

Craig said: "When he told me the price he'd paid I instantly knew they were either stolen or counterfeit and when he showed me a pack I quickly realised they were fake.

"That led to a very serious problem at the time with police raiding our homes and confiscating our passports while they investigated. In the end that cost us around £100,000 in paying fines, refunding Morrisons their money and losing out on what we'd paid out for them in the first place, not to mention legal bills. It wiped out most of that year's profit, in around 1995.

"Needless to say, Dad wasn't allowed to act as buyer ever again."

The business had outgrown its Brighouse base and the first thoughts were to relocate back to Huddersfield but this ended up being fraught with problems.

"We were always forward-thinking and future-proofing the business," said Craig. "By the mid-1990s we wanted to expand and were looking at a site on the retail park off Bradley Road but we weren't getting it at a decent price and there were protests against us moving there.

"We looked further afield and spotted a site being redeveloped just off junction 37 at the M1. It was cheaper than Huddersfield, grants were available as it was an old pit site and the council was incredibly positive and helpful, so we went there and the business quickly doubled in size from 35 to 70 employees."

Galpharm's strength was its ability to stay out in front of its competitors so it got its own products licences for paracetamol, aspirin and ibuprofen through the Medicines Control Agency. This meant it could use those licences to manufacture anywhere in the world – places which were far more cost-effective than the UK.

Craig said: "Our competitors were starting to catch us up but were all manufacturing in the UK. The race was to have the cheapest price which is why we took our manufacturing to India and, in the end, used four manufacturing sites over there.

"But they had to meet UK standards in terms of the production and the quality of the product so we constantly had our technical teams in India making sure that happened and the Medicines Control Agency also sent its inspectors out there."

The move made Galpharm unbeatable and it was a clear leader in own brand labels for several medicines.

Craig said: "Without some brilliant people in the business and without their skills and hard work we would not have achieved half of the success Galpharm went on to achieve. After we sold the business every one of the senior management team went on to be successful either in multi-nationals or their own businesses."

Craig says working with Graham can have its frustrations.

"I'd go so far as to say my dad's a genius but, like all geniuses, can be frustrating to work alongside. He's a classic entrepreneur who comes up with 10 ideas but only one of them will be ultimately feasible. But that idea will be something no-one else has thought of doing, not in a million years.

"Some people describe him as a butterfly who comes up with the idea and once he's got it up and running he's off doing something else.

"But there's no better frontman. He's a great character who will not stay in a box or be pigeon-holed.

"He's also one of those naturally lucky people. For instance, he wasn't wanting to sell Galpharm when we did. There was a lot of discussion and heartache about it, but we did eventually sell it, yet three months later the world economic crash hit us so even if we'd been able to sell it then the price wouldn't have been the same."

Craig and Graham bought well-known Huddersfield pub The Woodman at Thunderbridge and transformed it into one of the north's top wedding venues with around 100 weddings a year and 20 bedrooms run by Craig and his wife, Sarah, until they sold it in June 2022.

Both Graham and Craig played football for Wooldale Wanderers in the 1980s, including a couple of seasons together with Graham at right back and Craig on the right wing.

Craig went on to play for Shelley FC for 20 years, eventually became chairman and was friendly with Ash Berry who was a professional coach for junior teams at Huddersfield and Leeds.

Shelley only had two adult teams but Craig and Ash wanted to do far more for the community so looked for a new home for the team and Graham suggested the Storthes Hall campus where the University of Huddersfield had some pitches it no longer needed.

Craig also set up the Leslie Sports Foundation, a not-for-profit charity which has provided a base for hundreds of children each weekend and is the home pitch for Huddersfield Town Women FC and Huddersfield Dragons Hockey Club. Graham is a trustee for the charity.

The site was landlocked by other landowners and also the Government was involved as Storthes Hall was a former hospital for the mentally ill, but after two years of negotiations Craig secured a 99-year lease and pumped £500,000 into it which was match-funded by the Football Association and other pots of money along with great support from Kirklees Council.

They've redeveloped the whole site into a community sports hub, rebuilt the clubhouse, installed floodlights and it now has a first team pitch along with five other pitches and an all-weather pitch to become one of the biggest sports complexes in the area.

Shelley FC now has 23 teams – 20 of them for children – and youngsters come from all over Huddersfield, including some of its most deprived areas, to play football in a fantastic countryside setting.

Craig said: "Ash heads it up and the entire complex and the teams are run by amazing volunteers which is so humbling to see. On a Saturday morning the place is alive with hundreds of children playing football and Shelley FC has grown from a village team to one of the largest amateur football clubs in Yorkshire, set up to provide football for players of all abilities and all playing on decent, flat pitches."

And here's his final thoughts on his dad.

Craig, who now has an extensive property portfolio, said: "Graham's one of life's good guys who has led an incredibly interesting life. He really will do anything for anybody and, although it can be hard to work with him, if the 'proverbial' hits the fan he'll be there for you."

Amanda Chapman is Graham's daughter with first wife Sandra and was born in 1969

Amanda has lived in Ripon, North Yorkshire, for 30 years on a working farm with husband Chris and they have two grown-up daughters, Jordan and Madison.

She remembers helping Graham to pack boxes of pharmaceuticals first at Holmfirth and then at Firth Street.

She says: "As Mum and Dad had divorced I often saw him at weekends and he'd take me horse-riding on Saturdays and later on I'd then go and watch him play football and enjoy listening to the banter of his team-mates in the club afterwards while eating a pickled egg and drinking a dandelion & burdock.

"I fondly remember weekends away in the Lake District with Dad's little Shakespeare speed boat, learning to waterski and boogie boarding.

"He lived at Dog Kennel Bank at the time where he taught me important life skills such as eating cold baked beans out of a can and burning fish fingers on the grill.

"I was always welcome to take friends round. He was always playing his guitar, singing and was such a sociable guy."

Amanda has had several jobs including as an air stewardess and working in advertising and in a veterinary practice.

"Dad's always been very encouraging and motivational, so much so I grew up thinking I could do anything," she said. "He's kind, funny, great company and overly generous and he's always so optimistic. We all get a text from him every Monday morning saying 'Happy Monday' no matter how miserable the weather might be.

"Even now he's still busy working and I guess that ethic stretches back to his childhood and upbringing.

"We all love him dearly for all his quirks."

Alex Leslie is Graham's son to second wife Ann and now runs his own property development and real estate investment company

Alex, a married father-of-four, says his dad can have a wicked sense of humour, never more so than when he'd badly injured his leg.

In 2016 Alex jumped off a small bridge into a swimming pool, but unfortunately it was shallower than he thought and he broke 53 bones in his right foot, ankle and lower leg.

He underwent several operations and when he came round from one of the surgeries Graham had been out shopping for a present and appeared at the bottom of Alex's bed with it.

"It was probably the most inappropriate gift he could have given me," said Alex. "Yet his wicked smile said it all. He was clutching a pair of new shoes even though he knew I wouldn't be walking again for months.

"I regard him as my best friend and he's always there for me, be that for my achievements or if I'm feeling crushed and down.

"Dad has been an integral part of my life, offering unwavering support and guidance in both business and personal matters.

"In terms of his personality Dad possesses a unique blend of traits that make him truly remarkable. His unwavering optimism and resilience have been a source of inspiration for me during challenging times yet he has the ability to find joy in the simplest of moments.

"He has helped shape and guide me to be a better son, brother, father and husband. His values are his ultimate compass and he can always be depended on for guidance when the decisions aren't obvious and the direction isn't clear."

Fay Briddon is Graham's daughter to second wife Ann and was born in 1988

"My dad has always been a very hardworking man and he's alive when he's being creative. It was never about making money; it was about seeing an opportunity that no-one else had, it was about succeeding where others had failed and it was about creating something beautiful that would benefit his community and, later, his country.

"As I reached my teens my dad's success was sky rocketing and I remember feeling that the people around him had changed. The Arthur Haighs and Melvyn Hoyles from my childhood had been replaced by people with insincere smiles; you know the sort of smiles that don't reach the eyes.

"I've always wanted people to be around my dad for the right reasons but money does affect people in many different ways. It must have been – and still must be – hard for him to know if people's actions and words are from the right place."

She said Graham has always been a strong character.

"Bullying at school became rife as my dad turned up to collect us sometimes in a Ferrari or a Hummer," she said. "I used to get so embarrassed and angry with him. The school advised my dad that he should park down the road so the cars weren't seen by other children and parents. I will forever be grateful now to my dad for telling the school where they could put that idea. He taught me a valuable lesson – don't ever hide who you are. Be proud of yourself. Don't be afraid to be different.

"As a child I was petrified of the dark. I hated when night time was drawing in. One evening I couldn't sleep and remember my dad walking me outside into the garden. He had a big mug of tea and I could see the steam rising off it as I clung to his arm.

"The dark was so daunting and vast. He got to the centre of the lawn, stopped and said: 'Look up.' The sky was full of stars; it was beautiful.

"'How can that be scary?' he said. 'They never go away, they're always there over the top of us.'

"To this day if ever I feel lost, scared or sad I just look up. It's my comfort blanket. I did the same thing with my daughter when she was three years old and now she's obsessed with space and stars.

"When it comes to telling stories there's no-one better than my dad. He is a true salesman. I have a bell now. It's a 'bullshit bell'. It was actually bought for me by my dad should a story begin to make me feel like I'd just stepped into Narnia, I would 'ding' the bell. Myself and Karen will always give him the opportunity to provide evidence to support his tale but if none is forthcoming then the story has to return to fact.

"As a kid I remember I'd competed in a local showjumping competition one weekend and won. By Monday he'd told his colleagues I was the Junior National Showjumping Champion!

"To many people he is Professor Graham Leslie, to some he is Graham Leslie CBE and to others he is simply Graham. I am honoured and proud to call him Dad. My dad is an unbelievable human being; no, literally, unbelievable."

Graham's Huddersfield Town and stadium years ... here are the thoughts of stadium architect Rod Sheard, Sir John Harman, Paul Fletcher, Andy Booth, Peter Jackson, Steve Kindon, Kieran O'Regan, Ann Hough, Andy Hobson, Mel Booth and John Gledhill

Rod Sheard was the architect who led the design team for the new stadium and went on to play leading roles in designs for the new Wembley Stadium in London and the Millennium Stadium in Cardiff

In his book, *Sports Architecture*, Rod Sheard praises Graham as a man of vision.

He wrote that by the 1970s Huddersfield Town's old Leeds Road ground had "deteriorated into a shabby, unsafe and loss-making venue, attracting fewer than 8,000 spectators to the club's matches in the Football League's Third Division.

"If both the club and its stadium were to have any chance of survival, let alone progress, clearly radical action was sorely needed.

"Fortunately the club chairman during the early 1990s, Graham Leslie, was a man of vision and was able to inspire John Harman, leader of the local Kirklees Metropolitan Council, to join him. Together they took a leap into the future by forging a bold partnership between the football club, Huddersfield Rugby League Football Club and the local council to form a new company, Kirklees Stadium Development Ltd.

"The aim of this company was to plan, develop, own and manage a commercially viable, multi-use venue for soccer, rugby and other sports, social and community events, which would benefit all three owners.

"A brief was developed by the team including facilities which had never before been associated with a lower division football or rugby club. The words 'build it and they will come' summed up the spirit of positive thinking which pervaded every aspect of the development."

Rod added: "Since its opening the stadium has met its client's intention of becoming a landmark venue attracting sustained international publicity and winning a number of design awards. Since its opening, spectator attendance has doubled that of previous years and Huddersfield Town has maintained their position in a higher division of the football league. Huddersfield Rugby League Club has also been promoted and greatly increased attendance.

"The stadium's innovative design has also encouraged other

British sports clubs, towns and cities to aim higher in their efforts to replace ageing facilities."

Sir John Harman was the leader of Kirklees Council from 1986 to 1999 and was then chairman of the Environment Agency for eight years

Sir John says Graham was the man with the vision and determination to get the stadium project up and running.

He said: "When the idea for the new stadium was first mooted everyone said it wouldn't work but, as I saw it, there was no alternative. The old Leeds Road football ground was ramshackle and parts of the rugby ground had been declared unsafe with the club facing administration.

"After the Bradford City fire and the Hillsborough disaster it was evident this was a moment in history when things had to change. The Safety of Sports Grounds legislation had rightly been tightened and the Leeds Road ground was in a precarious if not untenable state and the Fartown rugby ground was getting into a condition where it wouldn't get a licence at all.

"When Graham came to see me in my office with his vision for a new stadium I was very struck at how open he was as to how we could work together to achieve it. His commitment was clear and he said the stadium absolutely had to be built. Personality and human relationships count for a lot and there was a high degree of trust here right from the start.

"Graham was only Huddersfield Town chairman for a short period but in that time he managed to get the Town board to commit to selling the old ground before they knew there was another place to go. It was a huge leap of faith and a significant risk for the club and I never underestimated what Graham had to do to get that over the line. It took phenomenal leadership.

"He has always had an unquenchable store of determination to make things happen and he was a prime mover in getting the deal in place which got the project underway. We pooled resources and agreed a fair ownership structure of 40% Kirklees Council, 40% the football club and 20% the rugby club.

That meant the partners had to work together and it is important to recognise that this balance is still in place and why. Graham put the project in motion. He lit the blue touchpaper and once that was burning there was no turning back.

"It was also a great deal in terms of what we got for the money. The contractors Alfred McAlpine must have worked on a narrow margin and the stadium which then bore the McAlpine name became a showcase for them to pitch for other major stadium-building projects. It was inspiring for many other clubs in the UK.

"It also came at a tough time economically when it was felt Huddersfield was on its knees and was symbolic in challenging the stereotype of Huddersfield as a place of flat caps and mill chimneys but a place of economic confidence that could produce what was later declared Building of the Year.

"I recognise what the football club means to the town's identity. If you ask people around the country what Huddersfield means to them they'll mention three things – Huddersfield town, Huddersfield Choral Society and textiles.

"The new stadium showed Huddersfield had turned a corner after some very tough times in the 80s and early 90s, it was the first of a new generation of stadium designs in the UK, the first stadium designed for shared use by football and rugby clubs and the first time a local authority and a football club had gone into a long-term commercial partnership for the good of the club and the town.

"Now we couldn't imagine the town without it."

Paul Fletcher was Huddersfield Town's commercial manager and then headed up the stadium's construction before becoming an acclaimed expert in stadium design and was commercial director for the new Wembley Stadium

Paul and Graham worked closely together to drive Huddersfield Town forward.

In his book *Magical Life in Football*, Paul describes Graham as a "dynamic chairman" who made him think very differently as he'd taken the commercial job on the understanding he'd not be involved in the new stadium. Graham quickly changed that.

Paul said: "Graham Leslie took control and his first instruction to me was, 'It's your job to build a new stadium for the club.' There was no refusal. I had to get a new stadium built and didn't know the first thing about it. I'd left school without an A-level or a spirit level. It can only have been the magnetism and drive of Graham Leslie that got me involved.

"Graham was a strong driving force. He had a clear vision, knew what he wanted and knew how to achieve it. He was also a supporter of the Terriers."

Paul said it would have been easy for Town to have looked at small capacity grounds but it would have meant the club would have remained in the lower divisions. Graham always thought big and had great vision which is why they went off to Canada to look at the massive £400m SkyDome in Toronto and taken inspiration from its best bits.

Andy Booth is a Huddersfield Town footballing legend who played for the club in two spells between 1992 and 2009, scoring 150 goals, and is now the club's ambassador

Andy says the players thought the stadium would never happen ... but when it did it helped to transform the club's fortunes.

And he reveals that manager Neil Warnock damaged the stadium in frustration during the team's first ever home game.

Andy was just starting out in his playing career when Graham was a Town director and then chairman and says: "As a young pro you rarely got to meet the board or the chairman. There were no agents around then. It was a case of being offered a new contract and then sign it if you wanted to play for the club.

"I remember that in around 1992 all the players and staff in the club were called into the Greenall Suite and shown a model of a stadium in a glass cage. It was an incredible sight but not like any stadium we'd seen before as it was so futuristic. We left that meeting shaking our heads saying, 'It'll never happen, not in Huddersfield.'

"But when the building got underway our manager, Neil Warnock, took us over to the new stadium site every week and we sat in the stands watching the builders at work. Neil said it was to make us feel to be part of the stadium before we were going to play in it as it was to be our new spiritual home.

"In the first game we played against Wycombe Wanderers and the crowd was a virtual sell-out, double our normal attendances. Unfortunately, we were appalling in the first half and Neil went berserk at half-time. The ceilings in the changing rooms at the old Leeds Road stadium were quite high but Neil punched upwards in frustration and smashed his fist straight through the ceiling tiles in the new stadium's home dressing room. The tiles came crashing down on his head and we had to try our hardest not to laugh, especially as he was going mad at us.

"We never managed to get a goal back and lost that first game but went on to win many more and the stadium has ended up with a great atmosphere.

"As club ambassador I take people on tours of the stadium and it still looks futuristic and brand new now, 30 years after it was built. What a testament to those who had the vision to create it for Huddersfield in the first place. It was a magnificent achievement."

Andy added: "When I retired from playing in 2009 Graham was one of the first people to call me and ask if I needed any help and offered to mentor me in whatever I did next. That was incredibly thoughtful and typical Graham."

Peter Jackson, former Huddersfield Town captain who managed the team from 1996–99 and again from 2003–04

Peter remembers that Graham had him working in the club shop to help generate more income.

He says: "The money to keep the club going used to mainly come through the turnstiles but Graham was always on the lookout for commercial opportunities so he had players working in the club shop. I was there a couple of afternoons a week and loved it.

"I remember he also transformed an old boot room into a café on matchdays – I went in to warm up one day and found a load of folk in there drinking beer.

"Graham has always had great foresight as hospitality has now become absolutely massive in the game.

"He changed a lot of things like that by thinking ahead, no more so than with the stadium. At that time the old Leeds Road ground was falling to bits and the club needed someone to come in with the personality and enthusiasm to change everything. Graham was that person.

"The new stadium doubled crowds instantly and it also meant better players wanted to join the club. It's a fantastic stadium which became an inspiring place."

Peter adds: "I tend to know if I'll get on with someone very quickly and within seconds I knew I'd know Graham for a long time. He's a really good guy who has had a big impact on me and I think a lot about him."

Steve Kindon, Town legend and former player

Steve Kindon is a legendary Huddersfield Town striker, notching up more than 50 goals in less than two seasons with the club – 14 goals in his first 17 games – before a knee injury cut his career short in October 1981.

He was the football club's commercial manager from 1982 to 1987 when he first met Graham Leslie shortly after he'd set up Galpharm in part of an old mill near Huddersfield town centre.

Steve says: "I went there to try to sell him a match sponsorship deal but when I got there I was faced by Graham in a small, basic, whitewashed office and when I saw what he was managing director of thought he'd never be able to afford the deal.

"But Graham really wanted to support Town and said he'd do it ... so long as his son, Craig, could be mascot for the game. The deal was done."

When Graham became Huddersfield Town chairman he wanted to rally the fans to support the team and appeal to anyone who wanted to get involved in running the club to step forward. He asked for Steve's advice on what to say.

Steve said: "I told him speak the truth, speak up and clearly, don't make it too long and make sure you say what you mean. It was all his own thoughts and words but he had the good grace to phone me up and thank me for the advice afterwards.

"That's Graham, always amicable and willing. There's no edge to him. What you see is what you get. Most people think he's quiet and shy but once you get to know him you realise he's a bundle of fun. He's always coming up with new ideas and some can be quite scatty and won't work but he never stops thinking and some of those ideas have completely taken off and brought him great success.

"He's a very determined person. When the idea was first mooted for a new stadium a lot of people didn't want it and thought the money should be spent on players instead.

"Then there was a suggestion that the stadium should be built out of the town centre near the motorway at Cooper Bridge, but Graham quite rightly felt the stadium should be near the heart of Huddersfield, in the centre of its community to create a sense of togetherness.

"That's how it always used to be. When Mick Buxton was manager in the late 1970s and early 1980s players were only allowed to live within the area where *The Huddersfield Daily Examiner* newspaper was delivered. They had to be part of the community they represented on the pitch."

Steve says the stadium put Huddersfield on the sporting map, the crowds instantly increased and the team has had relative success ever since, including a couple of seasons in the Premier League.

"All I'll say is look at the teams from Yorkshire towns that didn't think differently and build a new stadium," says Steve. "Almost all are languishing in the lower leagues and some, such as Halifax and York, are no longer league clubs."

Steve says Town were short of money by the early 1990s and so he used an idea from Everton who arranged a fundraising match just after the season finished each May where 33 people could pay to play 30 minutes against Everton players. Each group of 11 would have 30 minutes and then the team would totally change for the next 11 who would play the 15 minutes either side of half time and then the final 11 who would play the last half hour.

A charity match against the Huddersfield players was arranged which was the last game ever played at Leeds Road in 1994 ... and Graham was quick to hand over his money to play to lead by example.

Out of that sprang an incredible team of ex Town players and managers who would play against local teams for £500 on their pitches ... and at the end of the game the money would go to a good cause in that area. The team included England international and Town stalwart Trevor Cherry and centre half Roy Ellam along with managers Mick Buxton, Steve Smith and assistant managers Jimmy Robson and John Haselden. In one game they even had ex-Everton and England striker Joe Royle upfront.

But what's Steve's quirkiest memory of Graham?

"He's the only guy I know who plays golf wearing cufflinks."

Former Huddersfield Town and Republic of Ireland international football player Kieran O'Regan was at Town in the early 1990s.
"It was like a breath of fresh air when Graham became a director. He was so forward-thinking and things started to happen such as a new shirt sponsor, Gola, with some funky new designs.

"You could see that Graham thought differently and had to work incredibly hard to encourage people to see things his way and that it was the right thing to do. Getting the stadium off the ground involved a huge domino effect bringing different organisations on board but Graham did all the pushing to get any barriers knocked down.

"He was massively instrumental in starting the process to getting the new stadium built. We certainly needed it as the old Leeds Road ground was getting into a terrible state. I remember coming back from an away game one night and walking down a corridor carrying the kit for the laundry room and the floor was covered in cockroaches.

"Graham had been very successful in business by this point and left no stone unturned in his passion to create the first new build all-seater stadium in the UK. It was an incredible achievement to come up with such a futuristic design that still looks so impressive today, especially when you think Town was struggling in the old third division when Graham was so vigorously promoting the idea.

"He not only had the vision but also the commercial experience, knowledge, drive and determination to make it happen and to make people think completely differently about what a modern stadium should be."

Ann Hough, former Operations Director at Huddersfield Town Football Club

Ann had been with the club for 30 years until 2024 and says Graham has made a huge difference to the Huddersfield community from his vision for the stadium through to his natural philanthropy.

She says: "Graham's certainly a larger-than-life character who always has a smile on his face and is so helpful to everyone he meets.

"He was always determined Huddersfield should have a new stadium ... and what a stadium it is. If the old Leeds Road ground had been renovated to make it all-seater it would have had room for just 9,000 supporters whereas the new stadium's capacity is 24,590.

"That was so forward-thinking and what makes it even more amazing is that it was built when the club was facing tough times financially and even had to sell striker Iwan Roberts in the 1993–94 season just to stay afloat.

"It was ahead of its time in so many ways, especially the stadium's banqueting suite which can take up to 400 people and to this day is the only one of its size in Kirklees, hosting dozens of events every year. In 1994 we had a stadium that was the envy of most other clubs in the football league and it's still iconic today.

"It's brought so much revenue into the town – we've had 4,000 away supporters for some matches – and apart from Town and the Giants has hosted concerts attracting up to 40,000-strong crowds, rugby league world cup games and England under-21 matches.

"I remember the old Leeds Road stadium which was ugly, freezing cold and had spiders everywhere. It was horrible.

"Apart from instigating the stadium, Graham has been a very good friend to it and the club over the years to the point that Galpharm sponsored it and many people even now still think of it as the Galpharm Stadium.

"If you look at the Leslie Sports Foundation at Storthes Hall you can instantly see by the quality and scale of the facilities just what Graham can do for the Huddersfield community and what a difference he's made to so many lives."

Andy Hobson, Chief Executive of marketing agency Fantastic Media

Andy met Graham as a 19-year-old student anxious to learn more about the plans for a new stadium in Huddersfield. He then went on to become intrinsically linked with the stadium and is now a director of its operations company Kirklees Stadium Development Ltd.

Andy said: "In the early 1990s I was a teenager doing a graphic advertising course at Batley Art College but was really interested in sports marketing and architecture so when Graham Leslie, who was then Town chairman, revealed that a new stadium was planned for Huddersfield my eyes lit up.

"He had a small office in the end house of a row of terraces on Leeds Road and I was so keen to learn more about the stadium I plucked up the courage to knock on the door one day and when Graham's secretary answered I asked if I could have a look at what was planned.

"If this had been a large corporation it would have ended there, probably abruptly. Rather than get anywhere near the plans, I'd have been asked to leave and probably escorted away.

"Although Graham's secretary hesitated momentarily, Graham appeared from a back room and said, 'Let him through. Come in, young man.'

"He didn't have to do that. I was a teenager who knew very little and had absolutely nothing to bring to the scheme in terms of expertise or investment but he talked so excitedly about his vision and plans. That's Graham who has a genuine, honest enthusiasm to treat everyone the same and the great, welcoming way he treated me that day has always stuck with me.

"The stadium was so futuristic it was unbelievable. Don't forget Huddersfield Town was stuck in the old third division and not doing that well so had no right to think it could build a new stadium, let alone one that would lead the way for several other sports stadiums and, ultimately, the new Wembley.

"Imagine a team in the current League One doing that now. They'd probably be laughed at but Graham's incredible enthusiasm and determination that the Town stadium should not be the usual, boring boxlike design meant he got this highly ambitious project off the ground and up and running.

"At that time Town was only getting around 5,000 fans through the turnstiles every week. After the new stadium opened that jumped to 11,000. It was a massive statement for the club and the town and Graham had that unshakeable confidence to put it on the map. He thought differently and he thought big. He believed that if you build it the supporters will come. And they did."

Andy then became linked to the stadium almost right from the start and, after a short time working in London, returned to his home in Mirfield and got a job working for the stadium's promotions company when it was built.

He went on to work as a project development manager for the new stadiums at Bolton and Wembley – both designed by architect Rod Sheard who was responsible for the game-changing plans for Huddersfield's stadium.

Andy formed Leeds-based marketing agency Fantastic Media 18 years ago and his company sponsored a stand at the stadium for 16 years.

Yet it all started with that knock on Graham's door.

Mel Booth was the *Huddersfield Examiner*'s Chief Football Writer from 1985 to 2006 and Sports Editor from 2006 to 2020.

Mel says the stadium may never have happened without Graham's vision and determination right at the very start of the project.

He says: "Graham was definitely the right man at the right time for Huddersfield Town and, while others like George Binns and Paul Fletcher later played significant roles in the stadium project, Graham was the driven, ambitious and forward-thinking individual who made it all happen.

"His ideas were formulated during the 1989–90 season, when Graham was in the process of joining the board at Town and the Leeds Road ground was in desperate need of an upgrade in the wake of the Taylor Report following the Hillsborough disaster.

"The old ground, much loved and cherished as the club's only home, was crumbling before everyone's eyes and the club – which had a long-term lease – could not raise the funds to bring it up to the standards required by the Taylor Report. It needed innovative action to address the problem and Graham came up with the answer.

"He sought the direct help of Kirklees Council leader John Harman (now Sir John) to help Graham develop the stadium idea and run with it to the benefit not only of Town but Huddersfield Giants who had played a couple of seasons of rugby league at Leeds Road and also the whole community, with a venue to stage major events.

"The plan was as good as it could be. With a site just across the road from the old ground there were no complaints from supporters that the stadium was nowhere near the old one (as happened at Bolton where they moved out of town).

"There were also no complaints from residents because they were already living near to the club's home. So it was all pretty seamless, apart from dealing with some old chemical and munitions problems on the new acreage.

"Kirklees Council played its part by allowing the old ground to be sold, providing funds for the stadium project (they could have told the club to stay where they were), and with other money being attracted along with council support, they were able to dig the first sod and get things under way.

"The stadium wasn't complete, of course, by the time the first match was played there in 1994 and Graham was no longer chairman or even on the board. But it was his vision coming to reality and, without his prompting and persuasion at the beginning, it may never have happened at all.

"The immediate benefit for Town was that their attendances pretty much doubled overnight. It helped that the first season at the stadium ended in promotion, but before leaving Leeds Road the club averaged around 6,000 for home crowds. Their first three seasons at the new stadium brought average crowds of 11,629, 13,124 and 12,119 and the trend continued. So the figures speak for themselves."

John Gledhill was the sports editor at *The Huddersfield Daily Examiner* when Graham Leslie was both Town chairman and prime mover behind the new stadium.

He said Graham's determination was vital in getting the new stadium off the ground.

John says: "There is no doubting that Graham's drive and enthusiasm provided the catalyst or spur for the creation of Kirklees Stadium – still the official title but with acknowledgement to sponsorship and currently named the John Smith's Stadium.

"Graham's vision for a new stadium to replace the old Leeds Road ground was not matched by others in the couple of years or so to the build-up of the opening in 1994.

"This was a continuing frustration for Graham, although during his time as chairman of Town he was to gain and acknowledge the valuable support provided by George Binns and Paul Fletcher within the club and also that of Sir John Harman, then leader of Kirklees Council.

"So, there was much hard work and enterprise needed with Graham's insatiable appetite for getting things done an integral part of the ambitious project which, once completed, produced something of a trail-blazer in the modern era of sports stadia.

"Honoured with a CBE in 2017, Graham, always with an infectious smile (or cheeky grin) is very much an unsung hero in terms of his quiet and unassuming support for various charities and individuals.

"Not bad for a dyslexic and one who took out a modest bank loan to launch a career in hairdressing when he left school – a shame he never got around to snipping Mel Booth's golden locks!"

Ken Davy is the chairman of Huddersfield Giants and founder of Huddersfield-based financial services company Fintel

Ken has known Graham for around 30 years.

He says: "His positive attitude has always shone through, along with his obvious boundless energy. Graham is one of those delightful individuals who, whenever or wherever you meet them, have the ability to make you feel better for having had the encounter.

"Having shared a platform with Graham it's fascinating to see the way he intrigues his audience by bringing a guitar onto the stage. He may not play it, but it certainly enables him to keep his audiences engaged.

"He has obviously also enjoyed significant success in business and in his many other interests. I'm sure he will always excel at whatever he chooses to turn his hand to."

The Galpharm years ... business associates lift the lid on working with Graham

Dennis Corson was regional manager at Winthrop pharmaceuticals who gave Graham his first job in the industry and Graham still calls him 'The Boss'

Dennis interviewed Graham back in 1972 when he applied for his first job in pharmaceuticals.

If he hadn't got the job as junior sales rep at Winthrop, the chances are he wouldn't have gone into the pharmaceutical industry at all and Galpharm would never have happened.

It was a major crossroads moment in his life, possibly *the* crossroads moment.

Dennis remembers it well, especially when he asked a young Graham Leslie about his over-riding ambition.

"He told me he wanted to own a Rolls Royce one day," said Dennis. "How could I forget that and that day certainly came. Graham came across as very positive and confident from the start and was always quick to see and seize opportunities.

"Despite all his success Graham's not changed, he's still the same lad I remember back then. He always stood out for his commitment and desire to succeed and was always very popular among his colleagues.

"When Graham set up on his own as Galpharm in the early 1980s he was taking a great risk in what was a competitive market and I admired his courage to take the plunge, but just look at the success he went on to have.

"Over the years he's created jobs for so many people both in the UK and overseas in countries like India. He also does a lot of good, charitable work behind the scenes without seeking publicity.

"The world would be a much better place if there were more people like Graham with his enthusiasm, kindness and desire to benefit mankind. He's a person who always puts more into what he organises than he ever takes out. It's my pleasure and privilege to have known him more than 50 years."

Richard Eggleston was the Director of Research and Development at Galpharm. He has held very senior positions at corporations such as Johnson and Johnson and now runs his own company, Approved Pharma Solutions Ltd, which develops niche medicines

for oncology, epilepsy and diabetes.

Richard went to see Graham in around 1999 when Galpharm and Johnson and Johnson were thinking of teaming up to bring a new brand of children's paracetamol to market.

That didn't come off but Graham was so impressed with Richard he offered him a role in Galpharm to lead the company's research and development.

Richard was already keen to explore the possibility of making more medicines easily accessible over the counter rather than prescription only, liked what he saw at Galpharm and thought, "Why not?"

Over the next eight years he totally revamped the quality management system at Galpharm, transforming it into one of the best in the world.

Galpharm was among the first to licence a pharmaceutical factory in India to British standards and by 2008 they had several manufacturers in India which has become one of the top pharmaceutical manufacturing countries in the world – in short, a pharmaceutical powerhouse.

The knock-on effect has been amazing.

Richard says: "By finding quality producers at such good value for money, Graham has saved the NHS billions of pounds and totally transformed how people buy medicines over the counter in the UK and, probably, other parts of the world too with many other countries following suit.

"Without Galpharm leading the way, people would still be waiting for chemists to open to get medicines such as hay fever tablets.

"The major products we provided so cost-effectively were pain-relieving analgesics such as paracetamol and ibuprofen, hay fever products and medications to help indigestion and heartburn or to stop diarrhoea.

"Graham's other great quality is finding the right people and then giving them the freedom to go and make a difference for Galpharm. He'd say to them, 'If you think you can do it, then go and do it.'

"It meant we led the way so many times. The first antibiotic people could buy over the counter came from Galpharm."

The Medicines and Healthcare Products Regulatory Agency regulates pharmaceuticals in the UK and goes out to check Indian companies are producing medicines that meet British standards. Galpharm sent its technical team out to the factories four times a year to constantly check that standards were maintained.

Licences are renewed every two years and Galpharm's rigorous checking meant they never lost a licence, although several rival companies who copied Galpharm and started to produce in India did lose theirs.

Richard adds: "When you go into supermarkets and corner shops to buy medicines remember they are now so easily accessible and affordable because of what Graham and Galpharm did."

Irwin Armstrong, chief executive of CIGA Healthcare, who worked with Graham during his Galpharm days

Irwin Armstrong is a well-known businessman in Northern Ireland who is chief executive of CIGA Healthcare which specialises in diagnostic tests for humans and animals under its Suresign brand name – and it all began after Graham had to turn down a business proposition.

CIGA, which now sells in 70 countries, began when Graham wanted to source supplies of pregnancy testing kits in 2004 and Irwin used his business contacts to find a Chinese-made product distributed through a company in California.

Graham was offered the sole distribution rights in the UK, but there was an issue with the patents at that time so Graham stepped back as he was thinking about selling Galpharm and Irwin stepped in. He needed to buy stock urgently and Graham immediately helped with a loan so Irwin decided to call the business CIGA which stands for Craig (Graham's son), Irwin, Graham and Armstrong and is also pronounced like the massive gaming and entertainment company Sega so people would remember it. There's some clever marketing in there too.

The company was founded in 2005 and has grown ever since, kick-started by Graham introducing CIGA to supermarket giant Asda, which took the product with Irwin following the Leslie business model of undercutting the rest of the market to an irresistible level. Most pregnancy testing kits at the time cost £2.99. CIGA's cost just 99p and that bold move cornered the market.

Graham and Irwin had first met in the mid-1980s when Irwin was running a disposable razor manufacturing business called Smart UK Ltd in Northern Ireland. Graham was searching for a manufacturer to make store brand razors and managed to get Irwin lots of business.

Irwin went on to shift his manufacturing to Bulgaria and later sold the business but the two remained friends. Irwin had been a business consultant for Galpharm in its very early years.

He says: "I gave Graham lots of advice but he never really listened to it. At one point he was working 80 hours a week as the only salesman in a staff of just three and I told him to take on another sales person. Graham insisted he could only find people who'd probably be half as good as himself at selling, but I pointed out it would still mean his sales would go up 50%.

"A few years later he was having problems within the company and sought my advice, so I went over, spoke to several people in the business and drew up a short report which started off with the name of a person who I thought should leave the business immediately.

"I faxed it through and Graham sent an employee to get it off the machine. Unfortunately it was the employee I'd advised him to sack.

"Graham is probably the best and most natural salesman I've ever met. To be a great salesman you need to get the potential buyer to like you and Graham's exceptionally good at putting people at their ease while building up a great working relationship with them.

"He always ends a business meeting by asking if there is anything else he can help the client with and that often explains why he's so successful. One buyer mentioned in passing he was having trouble locating lip balm. Some sales staff would take the easy option and simply say they don't stock or sell it.

"Not Graham. He then researched the market, found a lip balm manufacturer in Finland with a top-quality product at a good price and became one of the biggest providers of lip balm in the UK.

"He's not one for formal contracts, he prefers to build his business networks on trust in an honest and straightforward style. He's generous and kind, eager to help charities and to support family, friends and business acquaintances but certainly doesn't like those who take advantage of his good nature.

"Although on the outside he's incredibly social and a great extrovert, Graham's also complex and there's an introvert and quite a shy person in there too.

"In the 1980s and 90s he always stood out from the crowd with his sharp suits. The first time I saw him he wore a bright blue jacket, and the initial time I came over to Huddersfield, and Galpharm was just a corner spot in a large mill, he had a bright lime green chair. Fortunately I never saw him sitting in it while wearing his bright blue jacket. That would have been way too much."

What the academics think of Professor Graham Leslie at the University of Huddersfield

Professor Bob Cryan, University of Huddersfield Vice Chancellor
Bob believes Graham is such an inspirational figure in the business community for revolutionising the pharmaceutical industry he honoured him with a role which is thought to be the first of its kind in the UK and, quite possibly, the world.

He made Graham a Professor in Residence of Enterprise and Entrepreneurship which brought him into direct contact with students wanting to start out in business and provided a vital link between the university and the business community.

Graham is known for his generosity and gave the university £100,000 as part of a match-funding scheme with the government which brought in more than £1m to help disadvantaged students from poorer backgrounds. Many have been helped with £1,000 scholarships.

The scheme has meant a great deal to Bob who came from a similar background in Deighton, which is why he's so keen to help other young students starting out in life.

Bob said: "What I like about Graham is that he's so creative and energetic – there's something incredibly charming about him and when he donated that money to help less well-off students it brought me to tears. I think he actually agreed to it on his honeymoon.

"He's one of life's enthusiasts, always positive and supportive. I'm so pleased he was honoured with his CBE in 2017 and what he did with Galpharm was a gamechanger in how he made medicines such as paracetamol and ibuprofen both easily accessible and so very affordable, sometimes just 10% of what they'd been before.

"When I joined the university as Vice Chancellor in 2007 Graham had already been awarded an Honorary Doctorate the year before for his amazing business achievements. I immediately saw him as a very interesting character. He was regarded as something of a hero among the small and medium-sized business community and I was very keen to reach out to them to collaborate with the university and Graham was the natural choice to do so.

"A Professor in Residence would usually have academic qualifications but that's not the background Graham comes from and appointing him ultimately led to some great partnerships between the university and business, perhaps most notably Paxman Scalp Cooling and its pioneering work on preventing hair loss during cancer treatment.

"I wanted the university to go back to its roots. It began as a mechanical and scientific institute set up to support local industry which is exactly what I want the university to do now. Graham has helped me to achieve that and, with the 3M Buckley Innovation Centre, new businesses have been set up in this area."

Graham is on the 3M board and is renowned for giving inspirational talks to students at the university and supporting their start-up businesses, investing in some of them.

Bob added: "Graham totally changed the pharmaceutical industry for the common good and that's a very big contribution to society."

Professor Liz Towns-Andrews, Professor of Innovation at the University of Huddersfield, who set up the 3M Buckley Innovation Centre and was its chief executive

Liz set up the 3M Buckley Innovation Centre (BIC), securing £12m of European Regional Development funding and also organising the naming rights with multinational American company 3M.

It was established as a novel way of working between academia and industry so rather than 'spinning out' businesses from the university they 'spin them in', working closely with them to maximise their effectiveness and, ultimately, success.

The vast majority of businesses in Huddersfield are small or medium enterprises and by moving into the BIC can actively benefit from the university's technology, skills and equipment, such as 3D printers which would usually be way out of their price range to buy themselves. There's a big emphasis on engineering businesses which has traditionally been one of the town's great strengths.

Liz says research shows that businesses who work with both other businesses and higher education grow the fastest and those in the BIC rub shoulders with other innovative businesses in there while also benefiting from the university's resources and knowledge of other business support programmes.

Graham became involved with the BIC as Liz realised such a well-respected local entrepreneur would hugely benefit the 30 or so businesses in there and so he became an Entrepreneur in Residence with his own office.

He's made such a difference he's been honoured with a room named after him called The Graham Leslie Suite.

Liz said: "Graham has been able to give these businesses a real sense of what running your own company really involves. It's great to have a successful entrepreneur in the centre who has been there and done it. He's brought a whole different perspective and given a great deal of his time."

Liz says Graham mentored a new company called Red Kite Games until they outgrew the building and were eventually bought out by a large gaming company.

She said: "Graham is a lovely person with a fantastic sense of humour. When he tells people his personal story it's really engaging, gets their interest and retains it. I see him more as a friend now than a business acquaintance and if I needed advice about anything to do with business I'd seek his first."

Professor Andrew Ball, Pro Vice-Chancellor for Research and Enterprise at the University of Huddersfield

Andrew credits Graham with providing some great support to University of Huddersfield students.

He says: "Graham could have just sat back, relaxed and retired when he sold Galpharm but he's indefatigable, driven by a desire to keep learning and achieving in life. Anyone who meets him has to admire his tenacity. When most would just stop, he just keeps on going.

"He's so personable, easy to relate to and always helps people selflessly in respect of the time and effort he puts in. He's sponsored funds to help students in financial hardship and whenever he's in the 3M Buckley Innovation Centre next to the University of Huddersfield he has been an inspiration to the many start-up companies and student entrepreneurs in there. They really value having him around to advise them on how to launch their businesses.

"With so many business connections Graham has also brought the university lots of opportunities and partnerships such as our students getting work placements in the film and media industry, thanks to Graham's links with film-maker Ben Sweet and his company Film Buddy.

"Huddersfield company Innerva Shapemaster Global provides power-assisted exercise equipment for elderly and disabled people and is working with our healthcare department to study their healthcare benefits while Colt Precision is involved with the university's precision measurement laboratories which are one of the university's key strengths.

"Graham also introduced us to Benson Taylor, a phenomenal

musician who has become the university's composer in residence after working in Italy and Los Angeles, earning a reputation as one of the most exciting talents working in music for film, television and streaming services. His music has been featured in internationally-renowned dramas such as *Suits*, *Grey's Anatomy* and *Orange Is the New Black*."

People Graham has helped over the years share their thoughts

Peter Branson was the Prince's Trust regional director in Yorkshire from 2004 to 2010 and then became the first chief executive of the Forget Me Not Children's Hospice in Huddersfield

Peter first met Graham when he sat next to him at a business lunch in Leeds and, as the Prince's Trust regional director, asked if Graham could help the charity.

Peter says: "Graham said the most effective way to do that would be for him to encourage others in his business network to help but felt he needed some kind of authority to do that.

"So I made him the first ever regional ambassador for the Prince's Trust. The charity's chief executive found out about it, contacted me and said, 'We don't have regional ambassadors.' My reply was, 'Well, we do now.' And it turned out to be a great decision because Graham brought in several business people as Trust patrons and to become a patron the minimum donation at that time was £100,000.

"Graham was a massive support and through his contacts made a significant difference to the Prince's Trust funding in Yorkshire.

"When I left the Trust to become chief executive of the Forget Me Not Children's Hospice I phoned Graham to let him know and to thank him for all his help for the Trust. He then said he backed jockeys rather than horses and so became a great help at the hospice, again using his contacts to generate all kinds of support.

"He was instrumental in getting Princess Beatrice to become the hospice's Royal Patron.

"Graham has now become a firm friend and I've always admired his generosity in terms of giving his time and expertise whenever it's needed. I know I only have to pick up the phone and he'll be there to help."

Former Detective Chief Superintendent Chris Gregg headed up West Yorkshire Police's first specialist Homicide and Major Enquiry Team in West Yorkshire and then teamed up with one of the UK's top forensic scientists, Angela Gallop, and former Scotland Yard Commissioner Lord John Stevens to establish Axiom International Ltd which provides forensic science and operational policing services worldwide

Axiom has become a very well-known name in forensic science circles and, through working closely with the Foreign and Commonwealth Office, has provided training and programmes that build up the capabilities of forensic science and policing in countries including Iraq, Pakistan, Afghanistan, Bahrain, Nigeria, Somalia and Jordan.

But the company's success started at the University of Huddersfield when it ran a course to train 107 Libyan police officers in forensic science ... and Graham played an important role helping the university to host the course there.

Chris said: "Graham helped us massively by introducing us to the university and relationship building with the senior management team at the university who then felt confident to entrust us to be their partner.

"We were a strong team with mine and Lord Stevens's expertise in policing, Angela with a global reputation for forensic science and Graham with his business knowledge and his deep understanding of how academia and businesses working together can be hugely beneficial to both.

"Getting that initial partnership with the university set Axiom on its way and helped create our business model in developing police and forensic services overseas.

"Of the 107 officers, 78 graduated with Master of Science degrees, 14 went on to do PhDs and many are now in influential positions in the Libyan police force with the knowledge they learned in Huddersfield shared among many others.

"It was also the foundation for the current Libyan Forensic Service and a team went over there to help develop their forensic science laboratories. Up until then evidence was mainly through confession or eye-witness accounts and their justice system was very different."

Chris added: "We knew we needed a top academic partner for the course which is why we turned to Graham for his insight and experience and the university has a strong reputation for working with international students from all over the world.

"Operational experience was also important and we even set up a forensic science house on Firth Street next to the university where the students could learn and test their skills in a very realistic-looking setting.

"Police forces overseas want the gold standard when it comes to forensic science and police investigations. The UK has that standard which is why Axiom became such a success."

Richard Paxman, OBE, Chief Executive at Paxman Cooling which is the world-leading company for scalp-cooling during cancer treatment

"Graham has been both an inspiration and mentor throughout my career and continues to be. He has not only helped my personal development but had an influence on the direction of our company over the years, providing invaluable support.

"His kind, approachable manner has always impressed me, there to listen, ask questions and guide in a supportive way. He is a genuine and wonderful guy and I will always be grateful for all that he does, not only for Paxman and me but for so many others in business."

Tom Brooke is Graham's stepson who Graham helped with his fine food business

Tom is Graham's stepson who now runs two successful petrol stations and deli fine food stores in North Yorkshire – one on the A19 near York and the other on Darlington Road in Richmond – under the name Brooke's.

Tom graduated with a degree in Business Management and Finance at Northumbria University but says that may have taught him the theory but Graham helped to show him how to set up and run a business in practice which is very different and far more challenging than the textbooks suggest.

The petrol stations and shops were initially bought and renovated using Graham's pension fund with Tom paying monthly rent. By 2022 Tom was running the business so well he was able to buy the freehold back and is now the sole company director.

"I couldn't have done it without Graham," he said. "He has given me so much advice and support along the way. He was always there for me but also knows when to let go and let someone do it for themselves, learning from their own successes and mistakes. Everyone knows how enigmatic he can be, a person with real presence. I've learned so much from him and discovered how far removed running a business is from the textbooks to real life."

The York business was initially set up by Graham with Patrick Allen, former Director of Marketing at Co-operative Group, who was managing director of the 3M Buckley Innovation Centre in Huddersfield for two years from 2012 to 2014. Tom was doing analytical work for the 3M which is how they met.

Tom started out by doing analytical work for the business which was initially called Will and Freddies after Patrick's children and was then appointed business development manager to source suppliers and products. He became company director when Patrick stepped back from the business to pursue other opportunities.

Tom grasped the chance, renamed the York station Brooke's and then opened a second Brooke's in Richmond in 2016. There probably would have been a third by now if Covid hadn't got in the way.

Tom said: "Patrick and Graham had the initial idea to make deli stores attached to petrol stations a destination rather than just a stopping off place to buy fuel. It's certainly worked as we have so many loyal customers now at both."

The two businesses turn over around £8m and Tom employs almost 20 staff with the stores stocking thousands of items from more than 100 suppliers, selling mainly Yorkshire produce including pies, cheeses, charcuterie, craft beer and curries. Tom has even set up Brooke's own brand of gin.

And he's still in regular contact with Graham.

"He's always open and honest about what I should do whether I agree with his ideas or not," he said. "What's happened with Brooke's is classic Graham, helping so much to set up a fledgling business, supporting it to grow and then leaving the person in charge to run with it and take it on to further success. I can't speak highly enough of him."

Dr Matthew Brooke is Graham's stepson and a scientist at University College London

Matthew is currently the senior scientific coordinator of the NorthStar clinical network at the University College London Great Ormond Street Institute of Child Health. The NorthStar network is the world's largest natural history study of boys and men with Duchenne muscular dystrophy (DMD) and a network of UK-wide healthcare professionals focusing on the best clinical management of DMD.

He says: "Graham has been a great friend and mentor to me, personally and professionally.

"Everyone knows what a gregarious, generous personality he is in a crowded room, but he's also a kind, supportive family man who has helped me in countless ways since we first met.

"He's inquisitive, interested, keen to learn and is a great, relentless source of ideas. He can intuitively grasp complex problems and is unerring in his ability to home in on the key points.

"He has supported me throughout my research and career and has been a fantastic source of advice and a helpful sounding board who has been available any time I've needed him.

"Spending time with Graham is always a pleasure and he's very much loved by my family and I."